IT'S THEM, NOT YOU

IT'S THEM, NOT YOU

How to Break Free from Toxic Parents and Reclaim Your Story

JOSH CONNOLLY

Vermilion, an imprint of Ebury Publishing
20 Vauxhall Bridge Road
London SW1V 2SA

Vermilion is part of the Penguin Random House group of companies
whose addresses can be found at global.penguinrandomhouse.com

First published by Vermilion in 2024

www.penguin.co.uk

A CIP catalogue record for this book is available from the British Library

ISBN 9781785044847

Typeset in 11/17.3pt Adobe Caslon Pro by Jouve (UK), Milton Keynes
Printed and bound in Great Britain by Clays Ltd, Elcograf S.p.A.

The authorised representative in the EEA is Penguin Random House Ireland,
Morrison Chambers, 32 Nassau Street, Dublin D02 YH68

I would like to dedicate this to my wife and children, without whom this wouldn't be possible.

CONTENTS

Introduction 1

1. What Is a Toxic Parent? 11
2. Managing a Toxic Parent 38
3. Healing in Community 55
4. Body First 70
5. It Starts Now 94
6. Self-Compassion 116
7. Meeting Every Version of You 137
8. Healing Your Relationships 161
9. Bringing Home Your Inner Child 187
10. Reparenting Your Inner Child 196

Conclusion 213

Further Resources 219
Index 221
About the Author 231

INTRODUCTION

You feel desperately alone. You know something in your life isn't right, but you dare not speak it aloud. Deep within, you know that the relationship with the very person who is supposed to love you unconditionally is the one that makes you feel unlovable. You struggle to be truly present with your loved ones. You often feel like life is one big show and that you are just going along with it.

Sound familiar?

Picking up this book is the first, most important and perhaps the hardest step in your life, as you discover that you have the power to truly break free from your toxic parent and reclaim your story.

Somewhere down the line, whether you knew it or not, because of your relationship with a parent, both parents or a carer, you invented versions of yourself simply to survive. And today, you're still living out those characters to get by.

Maybe you play certain roles to make sure everyone else is

happy, but have no idea how to get your own needs met. Does this dynamic sound familiar?

Perhaps you're a 'people-pleaser' because you're constantly afraid of letting others down. Even in moments when you're supposed to be happy and fulfilled, you're only ever performing for those around you. There are parts of you that you hide deep inside of you, even keeping them from the closest people in your life. You desperately work hard to avoid an internal 'darkness' within yourself but you know it's always there. You have tried self-help work, you have read the books, signed up to the courses or followed the latest wellbeing trend to try and 'fix' what you believe is broken. Eventually, you resign yourself to the belief that 'it's just the way I am'. You might have convinced yourself that you are broken and beyond repair. After all, this is what most of society is telling you in one way or another.

> BUT YOU ARE NOT BROKEN. YOU ARE NOT BROKEN, AND YOU DO NOT NEED TO BE 'FIXED'.

What you need to do is to stop abandoning yourself to protect the family dysfunction. It's time to stop making excuses for all the things that weren't right in your relationships as you were growing up, and those that still aren't right now that you're an adult. This is where you will find the truest understanding of yourself. And then once you know how your past informs you, you can truly begin to champion your future self.

WHO AM I?

I have faced my own struggles. I was in a lot of darkness for most of my younger life. There were fun times and good memories during it too, so it wasn't easy to see at first. With the darkness, I simply took it as part and parcel of life. I didn't know any different and didn't know how to navigate it, so I just ignored it. I thought that I was broken, and that the dark parts of me were to be bypassed and avoided at all costs.

I began my healing journey over 11 years ago and, through it, I have learned that this 'way that I am' is the very thing that gives me the power to explore my darkness, to heal and to ultimately come to love what I always ran away from. I have dedicated the last decade to this work. At first for myself, but then to help others explore their healing journeys. I've been inspired by some incredibly wise people, and have explored many dead-ends along the way too. I have found all too often that what's offered is a quick fix or rapid transformation, where enlightenment and healing are promised, but which only leaves you stuck in your head.

This is where my practice and what you'll learn in this book will depart from the usual wellbeing practices you may be used to. Often, self-help borrows ideas from intellectual thinkers, without a focus on the most important person: you, the reader, and the person on this healing journey. It may feel that it's working for a bit, but it won't last. The truth is that you can't 'outsource' your healing by adopting someone else's quick fix.

I was once on a very different path and, following in the footsteps of a long family history of addiction and early death, was destined to become another statistic. In 2012, my life changed drastically when, at the age of 24, I decided to stop drinking alcohol, and embarked on a new journey of healing. In the years that followed I turned within and worked extensively on myself, and I continue to do so today. As a result of this work, I have become passionate about helping people in similar situations. Having learned how much my childhood has impacted who I am today, I realise I want to share the things that have helped change my life in such a drastic way.

Getting sober aged 24, I thought all my problems would disappear, but I quickly realised that quitting alcohol actually left me with my problems. I had convinced myself that all my struggles were born from my alcohol use, but sobriety quickly taught me that I had been using alcohol to supress all my difficult feelings. Without it, I was just left with them – and with no way to escape. That is where the journey to really understanding who I am began. It showed me why I'd acted the way that I had, and when I saw my experience in its entirety, so much of it made sense. I had grown up with an alcoholic father who I lost when I was very young, and I still have a close relationship with my mum, who has been a constant throughout my entire life. My knowledge of the struggles of living with a toxic parent come mainly from supporting other people in their experience, including people in my life that I have loved. Through my work that involves supporting people in a number of different ways, including as a helpline counsellor at Nacoa UK, the charity for whom I remain an ambassador to this day, to online programmes and over a decade of work within the healing space, I understand that blanket solutions of forgiving and forgetting don't work when trying to heal from toxicity and abuse within a family system. Through my thousands of online interactions, I clearly see that many people feel completely alone in this struggle. Most of them are forced into silence and feel they can't talk about it anywhere. I want this book to be the voice for people who have grown up in that toxicity, as well as help them find true healing.

I've worked to support individuals and groups of people looking to embark on their healing journey. From online community spaces and programmes to in-person workshops and one-on-one coaching, I now hold the belief that so many people's distress and struggle make absolute sense when you're willing to hold space long enough for them to explore their full experience.

I see clearly that there is a complete lack of space within our culture for people with a toxic parent to explore the difficult experiences that they have endured throughout their entire life. In fact, in nearly every case, most people either force children of toxic parents into loving and accepting their parents just as they are, or at best coax them onto a path towards forgiveness at the expense of themselves.

I am passionate about validating people's experiences, however difficult they are to hear. I run a programme for people from all over the world who have grown up with either a toxic parent or family dysfunction, aimed at beginning to help them heal from that childhood. I have seen countless people have life-changing experiences and truly begin to heal, understand exactly who they are in the world today and build a loving, nurturing and integrated relationship with themselves. I have discovered that reflective work, coupled with validation and an understanding of who you are in the world today, taken alongside somatic breathwork practices, can bring about life-changing experiences. I have witnessed it help thousands of people learn to love every single part of themselves and to recognise the power they already possess within them.

HOW TO USE THIS BOOK

My aim with this book is to first give you the validation that you both need and deserve, having grown up your whole life with a parent who shows up as toxic, and to take you through the healing process. I can help you do some of the true internal work that's needed in order to be able to heal from something that society still has no real understanding of.

I will talk about my healing journey only to help you understand what is possible, but with this book, my mission is to support you to discover your own healing power through your own authentic journey. I have supported thousands of people on their journey and have heard so many stories of people who have spent a lifetime desperately trying to hold on to a relationship with a parent who is consistently toxic. As a result, these people lose themselves.

I need you on my side. Once I've gained some of your trust and have helped validate your feelings by showing that I understand the situation that you've been through, I need you to put the work in. I will be asking you to do a lot of self-reflective work with pen and paper, as well as some breathwork exercises. As you work through this book, please ensure that you do the work that is listed here. I want to highlight that reading about the work is not the same as doing the work. I myself spent a lot of time as a falsely empowered person. I would read everything that I needed to read, listen to the podcasts, watch all the videos, and, because I knew I had all of the knowledge of what was needed, I could talk a good talk. I could share what people needed to do, but I hadn't done the work on myself. Thankfully, albeit through pain, I woke up to this fact and embarked on a journey with the work. Everything I ask you to do in this book is work that I have done and continue to do on myself.

Explore and be gentle with yourself, but do the exercises when you're able to. Someone once said there's a door that takes us to paradise and a door that takes us to read about paradise, and we're all stood at the door waiting to read about paradise. So many of us want the knowledge without doing the work but, if you are willing to do the work, you will get the outcomes from this book.

The breathwork practices will set this apart from any other journey you have been on and will make up a large part of the work that you will do throughout this book, specifically conscious connected breathing. For so many, this can be the missing piece of the puzzle. At the end of each chapter, you will see a QR code that will take you to a video guiding you through a breathwork experience that will end with a visualisation designed to conclude the work you do within that chapter. People have life-changing experiences after just one session, and I believe that with an open mind this can happen for you too. This part of the work is vital to the journey that you will go on. Though you may be thinking this is not for you, I will introduce it in a way that feels reachable to you and again ask that you keep an open mind and invite the potential of the breathwork in for you. At the end of each chapter, you will need to create space in your life to lie down and do this breathwork. I encourage you to do these exercises in the order they are laid out, as so much of the integration work that's needed comes with the breathwork experience. I hope that you'll keep an open mind and lean in to it as much as possible.

You're probably wondering how you heal from a toxic parent. This book will take you on that journey. I have taken countless people through this method over the years; it allows you to access your inner a child and become their champion.

Yes, inner child work is going to be a big part of this process, but not in the way you may have experienced before. Perhaps you've dabbled with inner child work in the past? Maybe you had positive experiences with it? Maybe it simply didn't work for you? Or maybe you even had experiences that were really negative and left you feeling worse than when you originally started? Most inner child work makes the mistake of diving straight back and trying to build a relationship with your inner child, and this completely ignores why you have disconnected from them in the first place. This is why the journey will start with who you are today and then journey backwards.

Chapters 1 to 4 will get you ready for the process. In Chapters 1 and 2 I'm going to help you understand exactly what a toxic parent is and how that relates to you. I will also give you some recommendations for managing your life today with a toxic parent. This will include getting clear on your boundaries. This is because the rest of this book will focus on dealing with the deeper internal wounds that have been created after a whole life at the hands of a toxic parent. It is about working on yourself and all of the things that you have some control over so that you can reclaim your power and live the life you were always meant to.

In Chapters 3 and 4 there are a couple of things that I want you to do in order to be fully ready for this process. Though Chapters 1 and 2 contain some reflective work, these are the chapters where you will truly begin to stretch outside of your comfort zone. From Chapter 5 the internal work truly begins, and what follows is developing self-compassion through some uncomfortable but meaningful reflective work. As you meet all of the versions of yourself, you are going to gain self-understanding beyond the realms of what you thought possible. Even before healing your relationships with the people that caused you so much of this distress. Finally, this journey will come to a close as you become your inner child's champion. Setting yourself free from the internal prison created by your toxic parent, you'll begin a new journey of reparenting yourself as a whole and connected person.

The work within this book is specifically designed to be done in chronological order. The tasks within each chapter will always build on your learning from the previous ones. As such, the exercises will not make sense as stand-alone pieces. Each chapter contains a range of reflective exercises to complete, from visualisations to journalling and breathwork. Once again, I encourage you to put your best effort into these. Some of them may feel new or outside your comfort zone – that is to be expected, but don't let it deter you from giving them your all. The temptation here is often to read each exercise, get a sense of its aim, brush over it in your head and then continue reading. Instead, be sure to pause at each exercise and gently encourage yourself to fully engage with it.

You're going to need to be gentle with yourself, too. This isn't a race, and this book is not a test in which you have to 'perform well'. It's something that will require you to create space in your life to do at a pace that suits you. There may be times when the work begins to feel overwhelming, in which case you can put the book down and come back to it later. It's OK to be nervous, it's OK to be scared and it's OK to sometimes push through both of those things, but we all have a limit. Life can feel overwhelming, particularly when you have suffered a dysfunctional upbringing, so look after yourself.

This is more than just a book; it is journey home to yourself. In writing it, my hope is that you will see and speak your truth, allowing yourself to be the centre of your world for a moment. Through that, you will discover how your life can change. I am simply here to cheer you on and show you that you can do this. But here's my warning: you will have to put in the work. You will go to places that you may have buried deep or didn't even know existed. I will communicate all my valuable learnings and research over the years, together with my experience doing this work with real people in the world. I hope the book will serve to both deepen your understanding of yourself and act as a practical guide if you are seeking some transformation in your life. With this book, I will help you to find some peace among the chaos that your family dysfunction continues to create.

I sincerely hope that you'll see new possibilities for yourself, open pathways to connect with things that are important to you, and learn to love every single part of yourself without the need to 'fix' anything.

I truly believe that deep within you, you know exactly what you need to reclaim your innate power – and this book will help you discover that!

1.
WHAT IS A TOXIC PARENT?

'Toxic parent'. The term alone is enough to make some people feel uneasy. Most can accept that there are toxic people, but the idea of a toxic parent is a step too far. This keeps those living with one alone and silent, all too aware of how unwilling or incapable people are to hear their truth.

'You only get one mum and dad.'

This commonly deployed sentence can cut short a conversation that, for so many, would shine light on a lifetime of suppression. It's also a sentence that prevents children of toxic parents from looking at their experience and making sense of their pain. For those who say it, it epitomises the inability to look truthfully at what causes so much of our distress. When people see or hear the truth of other people's pain, it holds a mirror up to their own – a mirror they would rather not face. Instead, people often opt for silver linings and fixed ideals about how we all *should* view our parents. It can seem like everyone is an expert at this, so terrified by the thought that a parent could be toxic that they prefer to reject the idea completely and instead offer 'perspective'.

All parents have failings; they all behave in ways that could be labelled as toxic. This makes people uncomfortable, even though it is a reality. So, rather than explore this painful reality, they will avoid it at all costs.

'Some people in the world have it way worse than you!'

Sound familiar?

Maybe it is true that there will always be someone who has it worse than you do, but that doesn't mean that what you feel right now isn't valid or as difficult as it feels. Don't get me wrong – I am fully aware of how useful perspective can be, but that isn't what we are talking about here. Perspective delivered in this way removes all context from your experience and says that your struggle is not valid simply because someone, somewhere, has it worse.

Life with a toxic parent runs deep. It seeps into every corner of your life, and it can be all-consuming; it goes beyond words. This isn't accidental, either. Toxic people are experts at ensuring that most of the control goes on just below the surface, making it almost impossible for you to communicate without seeming like the one 'overreacting'. Thus, you stay quiet, and so the cycle of control continues.

'Toxic parent' is not a fixed label. It doesn't come with a checklist whereby if your parent scores high enough, you can officially diagnose them as 'toxic'. In many ways it is a label unique to your own experience, and only you can decide if it is a term that you would want to use. If you believe that what you are experiencing is a toxic person, then that is your true experience. Nobody else gets to define that, and your view is also allowed to change, grow and evolve for you to see things in a new light just as you grow and evolve.

However, when I use the term 'toxic parent', I do so purposely because at the extreme end of the sliding scale sits a type of parent who for many is beyond comprehension. This is a type of parent that is worryingly more common than most would wish to believe. I am going to spend the next few pages highlighting some of the traits of your parent or parents when you were growing up and when you were a child. You will begin to recognise that it is almost as if they learned from the same textbook.

TRAITS OF TOXIC PARENTS

Controlling your emotions

'Don't be so ridiculous, you have no reason to feel upset!'

A toxic parent places themself at the centre of the universe and this is where they believe everybody else should place them as well. Their belief is that you exist simply to serve them. It may not be as conscious as that and they may not directly say this, but it is the reality of what they believe. As a result, the way that you express yourself will have been forced to fit exclusively around their needs. As a child, you were not allowed your feelings because your parent experienced those feelings as a direct attack on them, as if the existence of your feelings was a declaration that theirs didn't matter. It wasn't just the things your parent said, either. In fact, it may have been the way they were said, often accompanied by subtle changes in tone or in facial expressions that were almost impossible for you to vocalise. This would have added to your confusion. Your inability to articulate what you were sensing would have made you feel like you were making it up altogether.

This could happen with any and all of your emotions. In most cases it was impossible to tell how your parent would react to any emotional expression, but they would often have certain ones that they never allowed. For example, anger is one of the most common emotions that children of toxic parents are not allowed to express. Joy is another common one. It is certainly not limited to these two emotions. As I have said, most emotions expressed put you at risk of being shamed. Whenever your feelings did come up, it will have felt like you were burdening your parent as a result. Emotions were smothered and then shame was forced onto you for having such feelings, teaching you to hide them at all costs.

If you are wondering which emotions were most strongly contested by your parent, then reflect on those emotions you find most difficult to express in your life today – or even ones that you can't remember ever fully expressing. The emotions highlighted by this reflection will point to the feelings you were most fearful of expressing.

Even today you still feel that shame, as if you shouldn't feel the way you do. It could be because your parent is still in your life and still using their same tactics, or simply because the resulting internal wound is still there and you are still forced to drive your feelings back down into your body rather than expressing them authentically. You may feel that you have become completely detached from your feelings, making communicating your own needs impossible. This is something you will carry into all your relationships, believing that love means abandoning yourself to ensure that everyone else is OK. In fact, you may have built a whole personality on how useful you can be for others because that was the only way to experience love growing up.

Oversharing

'You are so mature for your age.'

You were likely told this as a child. Strangely, it is still seen as a compliment. You were forced to grow up fast for many reasons, not least because of some of the things your parent would tell you. It wouldn't have felt unusual at the time, but when you should have been lost in fairy tales you were already being pulled into adult drama.

At a very young age your parent will have begun sharing their life problems with you. They may have talked down about your other parent, citing how awful they were and listing all the ways they had been hurt by them, irrespective of whether they were still in a relationship with them or not. It will have made you feel a deep sense of responsibility for the parent imparting this information to you. You will have been desperate not to burden them with any of your worries. You will have felt torn about how you should behave to the other parent, feeling that if you expressed any positive feeling towards them you will have betrayed your toxic parent. They may even explicitly label you as a 'traitor' or 'two-faced' for showing the other parent any attention. This can have a huge impact on the family system, creating conflict that often only plays out below the surface.

Your toxic parent will also have spoken to you like you were a peer of their own age, establishing an inappropriate bond more suited to an adult friendship. Rarely would they even acknowledge that you had a life beyond what they experienced. When they arrange time together it is for them to emotionally vomit on you. Many a time you have been left confused and angry after being on the receiving end of one of your toxic parent's monologues. They may have come out of nowhere but are particularly bad on the numerous occasions they feel you have wronged them.

Most interactions with them will be more like a stream of consciousness that they dump on you. Conversations are not about interacting, but simply about them verbally spewing what they feel they need to. If the interaction is verbal, there will be no space for you to communicate any of your thoughts; it will be them speaking at you. If it is written, say in a text message, it is going to be very long. It will go off on a whole host of tangents, bringing up events from the past that hold no apparent relevance whatsoever. They will bamboozle you and pull you into their chaos. This is how they suck you in and, before you know it, you are tangled up in their web of dysfunction, defending things you have no need to defend. This can make laying any kind of boundary extremely difficult as it is their way of pulling you back in.

This still impacts you as an adult, and you still make decisions with your parent's wishes in mind. How you dress, the house you live in or even the romantic partner you pick can be impacted by the fear of what your toxic parent might think.

Gaslighting

'What's wrong with me? Why am I like this?!'

There were times when you would sit alone in your room, confused and desperately questioning yourself. You were learning that you couldn't trust the way you felt as your reality was always questioned or completely denied. You were repeatedly told that you behaved in a way or were feeling something that you could have sworn wasn't true.

Gaslighting is a favoured weapon of the toxic parent and a common thread throughout all of their behaviours. Their use of it is so powerful that you will constantly question your reality. When you call them out, they will deny it. You could literally show them a message they sent you from their phone, and they will flatly deny its existence. It is incredibly confusing and debilitating, and is a powerful weapon of control that makes you constantly question your truth.

It is embedded deeply, over time. When you were very small, they will have continually told you that they know you better than anyone. They would suggest that they can read your mind in an attempt to control how you think.

It will play a huge part in why you find it so hard to trust yourself. Your parent would tell you that you had done certain things, and you will have been so confused growing up as to why you couldn't remember doing so. They will have bent the truth to suit their narrative. Your memories of the exact sequence of certain events would be so far removed from their portrayal by your parent that trusting yourself feels impossible. For example, you may recall your parent being very stressed and angry during an event, and they will recall it as a moment only filled with joy.

With your reality so regularly denied, you will have felt stupid, defective or like a fraud. This is a breeding ground for shame. You may have felt like a 'naughty kid' and either played out that role or been confused as to why you felt so naughty despite not getting into much trouble outside of home. It is common for children to label themselves with words like 'naughty' or 'bad' because they simply don't have the capacity to zoom out and see reality.

Today, you likely gaslight yourself a lot, regularly denying your own reality or questioning your own motives. Trusting yourself and others at face value is almost impossible, and so more often than not you opt to stay protected and never let people see the real you.

Jealousy and resentment

Despite your constant attempts to demonstrate your value, nothing you've done has ever been good enough. Not the aced exam, the successful job application or even the announcement of a new relationship could pass without a comment that would pierce through and spoil your special moment.

Your toxic parent was jealous and resentful of you. Rather than supporting you and cultivating an environment that would harbour your success, they would do the opposite unless it fell in line with exactly what they believed you should be doing. Remember, they believe themself to be the centre of the universe and so, in their mind, there was a very specific life path that you were to follow. If you deviated from that, they would become resentful or jealous. They would put you down and make you feel big-headed for even contemplating celebrating your success outside of their desired path. Even if your success was within their desired path, the put-downs would still come, though much more snidely.

So much of this was and is about how they were perceived by others. A lot of the put-downs would come from concerns about how other people would view them as a result of what you had done. You may have found that they were aware enough to hide or disguise their jealousy and resentment in any public forum, often saving their jealous outbursts for times when they wouldn't be at risk of judgement from anyone else.

As your teenage years and puberty came along, jealousy of your appearance and social status will have gone up dramatically. If you were a girl and your toxic parent was your mother, you will have been called a 'slut', 'slag' or words to that effect. Attempts to control or completely restrict your social circle will have been common, regardless of whether it was your mother or father who was toxic. They will have had strong opinions on what you wore in terms of clothes and makeup, opinions that were often completely hypocritical when put in the context of what they themself would wear. Comments may not have always been as overt as 'slut', but regular underhand comments disguised as jokes will have been the norm.

You began to feel like if you did anything, it took up too much space, as if your very existence was an issue. You would then be constantly full of fear about what you said or did. You made yourself small at home because you had to. If success did come, your parent would celebrate it in public and say the most amazing things about you, while behind closed doors ensure you didn't get 'too big for your boots'.

As a result, you may have played small a lot of your life, or have obsessively tried to achieve big, subconsciously hoping that the next rung on the ladder would finally bring your parent's approval. Both responses make sense, but they both also kept you hidden and off the radar for support. If you became the one who obsessively achieved, then nobody at school questioned why that was. In fact, you may even have heard compliments being given to your toxic parent for the amazing job they'd done! Now, in adulthood, you might feel incredibly guilty that you have everything you wanted and yet still feel like something is missing. If you played it small in order to hide, then you became well versed at avoiding detection by anyone. You may even be celebrated for being so easy-going.

Ulterior motives

At first, every time your parent did something nice, such as arranging an activity together or buying a gift that you had wanted, it would create hope. Hope that somewhere in them was a loving and empathetic person that wanted to make you happy. Time and time again the small flame of hope was lit, only to be quickly extinguished. You may not yet be fully able to accept the realisation that there is always an alternative motive. Everything a toxic parent does is for their own gain and is always later weaponised against you, in moments when they scold and shout, 'After everything I did for you!' These moments also become ammunition in the smear campaign, which we will explore later.

As a result, you have struggled with people doing nice things for you. When someone does something kind for you, the anxiety kicks in. You become either desperately uncomfortable or scramble to understand what their motive is for being so nice. You can deal with insults way more easily than compliments! You might even shut down interactions and relationships in which you are shown too much affection, because of the reaction it now triggers in you. Like most of these traits, this helps your parent to maintain a deep level of control over you.

Personal attacks

Throughout your childhood and still today, your parent regularly attacks your character. In public, these attacks are subtle so that if you react, you appear to be the crazy one. Other times, behind closed doors, the attacks would be explicit, including derogatory comments on your clothes, your appearance or your character. They still come as an adult. If you have called them out for it, then they will tend to try and stick to underhanded comments that they can then deny having spoken with any malice. They can't always keep up that act, though, and so the coldness and the direct nastiness are still a regular occurrence.

Their favourite way to attack your character is projection. You can almost guarantee that everything they have called you reflects themself. This is extremely confusing because it can seem so obvious to you that they are projecting, but they seem so sure of what they are saying. For example, they may act in a passive-aggressive way, and then call your response passive-aggressive. Or, dare I say, they have called you toxic a few times! This in part explains your lifetime of questioning yourself or feeling that your opinions and needs are of no value. If you are now a parent, you may spend too much time questioning whether you have become the toxic parent.

Unpredictable mood swings

You spent your childhood walking on eggshells.

Your toxic parent's mood changes in a heartbeat and with no rationale. You would walk home from school heavy with concern as to what mood you were going to come home to. Desperate for control, you would begin internally practising how to behave when you walked through the door. Some days they would seem bouncy and upbeat, while on others they would overflow with rage. There was never any rhyme or reason to this.

Far from being a sanctuary of safety, home was a place where you learned to tiptoe around, desperate not to be the reason your parent had an outburst. Your very existence became a threat. This happened for two main reasons: (1) your parent is so unpredictable and (2) they actively created this environment as way of maintaining control. They regularly threatened to take away things you really cared about. Sometimes they would follow through on the threats, other times they would be dropped. The unpredictability left you constantly checking your behaviour against the environment.

That feeling of unpredictability is still there, and it's not just when you are with your toxic parent, but in a lot of your day-to-day life. It becomes all-consuming and almost completely impossible to be yourself, especially if that toxic parent is actively in your life.

You developed hypervigilance as a coping mechanism, and this has likely stuck with you. You became an expert at reading minds. You learned to notice even the most subtle change in energy. The higher your natural sensitivity, the deeper your hypervigilance. You began to self-organise based on the vibe you picked up. You honed this skill growing up and have carried it with you at your own expense. Self-organising remains your problem today. Your issue is not that you remain so in tune with everyone's emotional state, but that, when you sense those states, you instantly take responsibility for them. This is what helped you survive growing up: you became the perfect sponge for you parent's emotional needs, and you carry that into all your personal relationships. You walk on eggshells now with those who don't need it, checking people's energy and showing up accordingly. It's exhausting.

Spiritual bypassing

Spiritual bypassing pertains to the use of practices seen as spiritual in order to avoid facing any unresolved issues or difficult emotional experiences. 'Toxic positivity' is currently the more widely used term for a version of spiritual bypassing, whereby people think that simply focusing on the positives will make all the difficult feelings disappear. Spiritual bypassing could be described as when people embody that as a practice. Imagine someone who is abusive to everyone in their house all day, yet thinks that burning sage to cleanse the space at the end of the day can solve the issue. You can bet your life there's a poster in the kitchen that reads 'Positive Vibes Only' which they point to when you react appropriately to one of their attacks. I say this in jest, but there is some truth to it. Their avoidance of reflecting inwardly at all costs is only manageable by bypassing true emotions.

If you grew up with any kind of faith or religion in the home, they will have used this to aid in their emotional avoidance and to force you into yours, reciting spiritual text and moulding it to fit their own warped narrative. Religion isn't essential, though; you may also find them posting some whimsical quote to Facebook about letting go despite how tightly wound they are. Air any grievances, and you are certain to be met with a monologue on forgiveness, even though they are full of resentment.

Witnessing how amazing your parent could appear to the outside world was arguably one of the biggest struggles you faced as a child. You would be happy when there was company, because it meant you got the nice version of your parent. However it was extremely confusing witnessing them act like this incredible person only to see the mask drop behind closed doors.

The toxic parent will work hard to be credible and charitable to people in all outward-facing areas of their life. They are often celebrated within their community and many of them are figuratively sitting in the lotus position, burning incense all day. Spiritual groups are often the perfect hiding places for these people. Many are also on social media acting like the spiritual gurus of our time. They are often waxing lyrical about forgiving, letting go and calming one's energy. It is not that any of these things are bad per se, but, if you know what the person is really like, it is enough to make you sick. As a result, you have dealt with people celebrating your parent for your entire life, and exclaiming how grateful you must feel to have such a wonderful parent. But they don't see what you see when the door closes at night. This can lead you to feel like you must be the problem.

Reactive abuse

Eventually, you can't take it anymore and, crying hysterically or screaming in anger (probably both), you finally reach your limit. That's when the reactive abuse begins.

'See, I said you were crazy!'

They will abuse you and then suggest that your reaction is the issue, and you should be able to 'just let it go'. This is reactive abuse. They will push and push until a reaction inevitably comes, and then that is used against you. Your words and actions will be taken as if they are out of the blue, and a reflection of your character. It can be really debilitating for you and make you feel shame for wholly appropriate reactions. If they can, they will try to push you to your limit in the company of others. When that's not possible, your reactions will still be noted and held against you. Somewhere down the line, your words will be weaponised against you. Some parents even film your outburst as evidence. Reactive abuse is something that becomes a lot more prominent as you move into your teenage years, a time in which you are more likely to react.

As you moved into adulthood you may have seen their behaviour more for what it is, and learned that they crave your reaction. Regardless, it is difficult to not react.

The smear campaign

This is a powerful form of abuse that sweeps over boundaries and seeps into every aspect of your life.

When you reached your teenage years and the toxic parent could sense you were seeing some of their behaviour for what it was, the seeds of the smear campaign would have been planted. This would have been done cleverly and implicitly at first. Friends of the family would have been told by your toxic parent that they were 'worried about you'. If there was a messy breakup between the parents, they might say that you are 'just like your mum/dad'. Those family friends might have tried to help by putting their arm around you and telling you what an amazing person your toxic parent is.

If, and when, you start to wake up and courageously put your needs first, the smear campaign will begin in full swing. Anyone and everyone will be fed a certain narrative about you, one that portrays your toxic parent as the innocent victim. They will often not explicitly put you down because this could make them look like 'the bad one'. Where possible, it will be more subtle. They will tell people that they are doing everything they can, but it's so hard when you don't want to see them. They will spin lines about how they have made their mistakes, but they've always tried their best.

Even if someone hasn't yet been on the receiving end of this campaign, you approach every interaction as if they have. This can isolate you and remove any trust you may have had for people in your life. Bumping into acquaintances, you will find yourself trying to counter a narrative they might not have even been fed through fear of the smear campaign. At worst, it can blacklist you from communities.

If you have no contact or even minimal contact, you may find that they still send birthday and Christmas cards. There is often some twist on this. They could be late, or barely say anything. They might send them to your children and not you. This is all an attempt to maintain some level of control, and no doubt so that they can use it in their narrative and share with people how they have 'sent cards every year so they know that I at least tried'. These are calculated tales because they tap into real-life experiences of people who might have genuinely been wronged. Anyone who's listening is therefore easily roped into their world of sorrow.

I think it is all too easy to suggest that if anyone was taken in by the smear campaign then they were never your friend in the first place. This may be true for some of your closer friends, but for others, the manipulation tactics will have been strong. It is often the case that removing yourself entirely from whole friendship and even family circles is the only option. It is the smear campaign that can really bring about the feeling of being the black sheep of the family.

Victim mentality

There have likely been times when you are the villain in your toxic parent's story of victimhood, especially if you have ever spoken the truth about any of the family dysfunction. But you have definitely listened for hours upon hours to accounts of how they have been a victim all their life; whether it is stories about your other parent, their latest partner or a friend who has wronged them, nobody has, in their minds, been treated as badly as they have.

Victim mentality encompasses who and what they are. It will be one of their favourite projections, too. They will often bemoan people for having a victim mentality while celebrating their courageous, brave and strong fight through their own experiences. You have probably been told by them on more than one occasion that you 'play the victim' – despite the fact that, because of them, you've never had to *play* it.

It is natural to feel like you're the victim from time to time, even when you might not be one. We can all have moments in our lives when we think, *Why me?!* Now and then, life does that to us. This is especially true when you have been the victim in so many ways for so long. This is wholly different to the way in which toxic people use it. For them, it is a full-time thing that ensures that they are the centre of the world they exist in.

No self-reflection

'Sorry' is not something you have ever heard your parent say, nor is it something you ever will. You may be clinging on to the tiniest bit of hope that an apology will come, but deep down, you know it isn't coming. You may have heard apologetic words spoken in one of their streams of consciousness, but never any reflection of any meaning. This is despite having every single fault of yours highlighted by them.

This is what I think really separates a toxic parent from the rest of the sliding scale: the fact that they will never, under any circumstances, self-reflect. There never has been and never will be any give and take. In their world, they are the centre, everything revolves around them and that is it. This means they are consistent in their toxicity forever and will never change. I don't say this lightly, and there is still part of me that screams that surely everyone has some hope of change, right?! But if they are the parent I have outlined here, my difficult belief is that they never will.

JOURNAL PROMPTS

Before you continue, take some time to reflect fully on the traits that you have just explored.

- Which of the above traits resonated most strongly with you?
- Can you describe the physical feelings in your body as you read them?
- If you had to name the three strongest emotions that came up when reading the traits, what would they be?

When reading these traits, it is natural to feel a mix of emotions. Even if you were already very aware of your childhood experiences, seeing them clearly written can still be an emotional experience. Maybe you are also a parent, and recognise some of the mentioned behaviour in yourself? My belief is that if we all look hard enough, this is the case for even the nicest person. So, be gentle with yourself. We are all working at it and trying to be better. Having one of these traits doesn't automatically make you toxic. There is nothing quite as bad as realising that you are showing up with some of the exact traits that you are trying to heal from. We all have a level of toxicity, but your awareness of it and the fact that it made you recoil and want to change separates you from the toxic parents I am talking about.

You may also have felt a weight being lifted off your shoulders, to finally have said some things out loud without any filter. Sadness, anger, pity, disgust, compassion ... as with all of the work you are beginning to embark on, all emotions are welcome here.

You may have also felt some resistance to what you read, or felt a need to defend your parent. This is totally understandable and is not something to kick back against, but something to just notice. To admit your parent's failings is not an act of betrayal, but to ignore them entirely is an act of self-betrayal. You may have been taught that to see someone's flaws and recognise their impact on you is equal to loving them less. This is false, and is in fact dysfunctional. It stems from the same place so much of this does: your interactions with your parent when you were young.

Children deserve to hear from their parent or another adult when their parent's behaviour is not great. If nothing else, it teaches them that, as human beings, we all have flaws. They need to have their resulting feelings validated too. If I lose my temper one day with my children and raise my voice, they deserve to hear that I was in the wrong and that how they felt as a result was justified. Most children don't get this at all. They are more likely to have their parent and other adults excuse the parent's behaviour at all costs. So children, who are naturally egocentric, will begin to make themselves the problem; they have no other choice.

Of course, everyone has failings, and nothing prepares anyone for becoming a parent. The reality is that no one is ever 'completely healed' and everyone will have experienced some level of dysfunction growing up. There is a broad scale of dysfunction. You will sit somewhere on it and you may find that, over time, you will move along it. When you find yourself with a toxic parent at the severe end of the scale, it is one of the most unrecognised and unsupported places to be. It may be hard for you to comprehend – you may find yourself thinking you are overreacting – and this will be further compounded by the messaging from everyone around you.

Most everyone will be willing to admit that horrible people exist. Yes, some may say that people themselves aren't horrible and that it's only their behaviour, but it is irrelevant. If you had someone in your life who was consistently and repeatedly nasty, everyone's advice would be to end that relationship. In fact, a lot of ill-informed people would claim that allowing the relationship to continue was in itself an act of weakness. Unless, of course, we are talking about that nasty person being your parent. Then, everyone gets uncomfortable and the advice changes from ending the relationship to saving it at all costs! Irrespective of whether that cost is your own sanity. All of a sudden, you are not weak for staying but you are weak for wanting to leave. The level of toxicity seems to hold no relevance, either. You are simply not allowed to even remotely explore the failings of your parent, let alone suggest that you have a toxic one.

'You should feel lucky you have a parent in your life.'

'Life is too short; you'll miss them when they're gone!'

And then arguably the most invalidating:

'They were only doing their best.'

Why would people respond this way? When they say these things while venomously attacking, either passively or otherwise, they are likely the very people that I am discussing. You probably know the ones; they don't just offer bad advice but attack you for even exploring this notion. Self-reflection is off the table, and saying things clearly and directly is not going to sit comfortably with them. Attack becomes their only form of defence.

For some it may simply be impossible to imagine that any parent could reach the level of toxicity that we are discussing. Perhaps this is the best reason. Why would anyone believe that a parent could stoop to the levels that I am suggesting?

Unfortunately, I think that we humans tend to be more complex than this, and the cynic in me questions if this is ever the only reason for it. Many would likely offer this as reasoning but on reflection, with enough courage and curiosity, I think they would find there is more to it.

Many are running from their own shadows. Perhaps they are parents themselves and so regularly fall short of the invisible parenting bar. They lie in bed at night on more occasions than they would like to admit, beating themselves up for their failings as a parent. Upon hearing that someone would talk down about a parent, or, heaven forbid, cut them out, that version of them activates. On some level it recoils in shame. Their devaluing response is to protect them from themselves. I am not for a second suggesting that they should recoil in shame – I think parenting is the hardest thing any of us will ever do – my point is simply that their response has almost nothing to do with you and absolutely everything to do with them, and their own natural and perhaps appropriate insecurities.

Some people are themselves trapped in the control of a toxic parent, and I feel the most compassion for these people. When hearing someone speak truth about a toxic parent, it is too painful for them to reflect. They are protecting themselves from a truth too painful to bear. You yourself may have been this person. Much like the parents reacting to their own insecurities, these people are keeping their own protective narrative safe.

Many people have trouble even acknowledging that toxic parents exist. This is why this difficult conversation really matters. At the heart of it is a deep-rooted shame that continues to pass through generations until someone is willing to see, process and release it in its entirety. This means speaking uncomfortable truths that most would rather leave neatly swept under the carpet.

After all, where do you go as a child if you have an emotionally abusive parent? At a young age, it is almost impossible to fully recognise and comprehend. But if you did, who would you turn to? Speak to an adult at school and the first thing they are going to do is contact the parent for a chat. Children know this, and so silence is the only option.

I often speak in school assemblies and my experience confirms this. I will share some of my stories about life with an alcoholic father. I can see the young people that it impacts. Some will look down, some will hold my gaze the entire session and some will start to play up and be silly. Often some students stay behind to talk to me. They are cryptic in the way they speak. They tell me I am just like them, or words to a similar effect. When I ask if they are talking to anyone about it, they say no, almost every time. When I ask why, the answer is always the same. They know that by speaking to me they risk it becoming a safeguarding issue. This would mean that I would need to report a concern, and then there is a duty to inform the parent or carer – their worst nightmare.

So, many children don't even come close to talking about their abuse. This may have been true for you. Instead, they begin a lifetime of self-abandonment and consider themselves responsible for the very person abusing them. They then carry this with them into adulthood, only ever holding themselves accountable, while repeatedly shaming themselves for doing so.

At its core, most healing work is about saying the unsaid and feeling the unfelt. That is why I am explicit with the term 'toxic parent', because I do believe that many of the parents I am talking about are toxic. This simply isn't talked about explicitly enough. In fact, it is actively ignored. So, if you have had a realisation of just how toxic your parent is, it is almost certain that they were the same way when you were growing up and you have never had your experience validated.

It could be that you only started to wake up to the true reality when you had your own children, or that over time you began to realise that so much of what you experienced was not right. You find yourself reciting a story about your childhood to someone, laughing as you do, only to realise that what you're saying isn't funny.

With this book, it is not my wish to make you see your parent as toxic, but I do want to validate your truth, whatever that is. There is a body of people much larger than we care to believe who hear the term 'toxic parent' and instantly get a sense that it describes their mum, dad, grandparent or carer to a T. There will be some more of you that, upon hearing some of the traits I have outlined, will have the same realisation. For an even larger group of people (dare I suggest most of us?), there will be some recognition of a level of dysfunction within their family. Power to you. That is not easy, and the process in this book is as much for you as it is for anyone else.

For some, comprehending no contact will be impossible. But for others, it will be the only option. I do not wish to have an opinion on anyone's situation as every single circumstance has common traits but comes with its own set of complexities. It is only for you to decide what works for you, and you are allowed to change your mind on that. I will, however, offer this analogy. How close to the fire can you sit without getting burned? It may be close, it may be that you need to get away entirely, or it may be that you switch between close and far depending on how you feel. It is your journey and your journey only. Try the best you can to ignore what people who haven't walked in your shoes think you should do and listen to your heart. I hope this book will help you with that.

If you have a toxic parent, you have probably tried everything possible to save that relationship. You may wish to continue on that journey of trying to save it. You may not. I also think it is too late to go back and live the perfect childhood, but wherever you find yourself now, you picked up this book because there is a part of you that believes you deserve more. Regardless of where you find yourself in your relationship with your parent, you deserve a shot at healing and a shot at life. You can achieve this if you are willing to courageously look within and do some of the work outlined in this book!

JOURNAL PROMPTS

Reflect on the questions below to help bring this first chapter to a close.

- How does it feel to see all of this information on toxic parents laid out?
- List some feelings that you have around starting this journey.
- Do you have any worries about embarking on this journey?

Breathwork

Before you head into the next chapter, it is time to introduce the breathwork that you will use on this journey. As mentioned in the introduction, breathwork will form a huge part of the work you will do. As you move through the chapters, the breathwork sessions alone have the potential to bring about huge life-changing experiences and, if you can keep an open mind and give them all a try, I believe they can do this for you too. You will begin in this chapter and the next three by gently leaning in to it and practising the technique. Follow the QR code below to try this gentle introduction breathwork session.

2. MANAGING A TOXIC PARENT

Life as an adult with a toxic parent can be all-consuming. Their incessant manipulation and desire to remain at the centre of the universe can take its toll on your mental, emotional and physical health.

The journey that you have begun with this book is about reclaiming the power taken from you as you grew through life at the hands of a toxic parent. A life that nothing or nobody can prepare you for and one that you didn't deserve. However, something that must be highlighted is that though you most certainly can and will reclaim your power, you cannot change your toxic parent and, in most cases, the difficult truth is that they won't ever change themself. This is going to mean that there will be situations and instances that you need to manage in the moment. Even if you have already reduced to zero contact, the attempt to still impact your life from afar will remain.

Within this chapter, I will highlight some typical scenarios that many adult children of a toxic parent will experience within adulthood, as well as introducing some tips for navigating them to have the least negative impact on your life today. I also want you to see that you are not overreacting; you are not going 'crazy', you are not alone, and that it is almost like toxic parents are all learning from the same textbook.

It is important to speak explicitly about what life can be like for people who live with a toxic parent. Their greatest secret weapon is society's silence. Society's total unwillingness to believe that any parent could be as toxic as some are. Society's seeming desire to push this all back under the carpet and continue operating under the facade that 'all parents are doing their best' and that is good enough. The reality for adult children of toxic parents is much more difficult, particularly when trying to maintain any kind of contact, however small. Confusion and questioning of one's own reality becomes a constant, and with no real space to explore that reality it can become a lonely place.

EXPERIENCES OF TOXIC PARENTING DURING ADULTHOOD

Random contact

This is when your toxic parent makes contact from nowhere, completely out of the blue. The contact may have no context whatsoever or may be in a completely different context to your current experience with them. For example, they may reach out with a loving interaction, telling you how much they love and care for you, despite it being a week since your last interaction that ended in a heated argument after they were extremely cruel. To the average person this may seem like the parent is simply extending an olive branch. You may find yourself wanting to believe this too, but the reality is that it is not that at all. Instead, it has a lot more to do with some of the traits you explored in the previous chapter. Predominately their belief that they should be the centre of the universe coupled with their complete lack of ability to self-reflect. There is almost always an ulterior motive designed to draw you back into the drama, or to simply create some kind of reaction that they can use against you. This contact is often in the form of a cryptic text message that leaves you questioning your reality, and means that if you do reply with anything remotely negative then you can be seen as the 'bad one'. The key in this instance is to not engage at all. If there is something particular or time-sensitive within their message that needs a response, then responding to only that, clearly and with no emotion, is the best and only option here.

'After everything I did for you!'

A sentence (along with others to the same effect) that every adult child of a toxic parent has heard more times than they can remember. Let me be clear here: all parents have likely said this or words to this effect at times. At the worst times, children *can* sometimes be ungrateful and, as a parent, I have found myself wanting to highlight to my own children some of the things they should be grateful for. What I am talking about in this instance is completely different. With a toxic parent this is constant and is used so often that, in the end, it shows that any time your parent does something good for you, it is certain to be weaponised and used against you in the future. It is your toxic parent believing that you should treat them exactly as they desire, irrespective of how they might be showing up for you.

They will cite having raised you while making sure you can see how hard it was for them and use that to guilt-trip you into doing and being whatever they want and need in that moment. In these instances, it pays to remind yourself that any so-called good deed they did and then later brought up to use against you means that they didn't do it for you in the first place at all, they did it for ammunition. I appreciate this is a cold and difficult truth, but I also recognise the relief that can come for many when they see it articulated so directly for the first time. If at all possible in your life today, avoid taking any favours from them at all. I also appreciate that this isn't always entirely possible. A common example might be the need for childcare. It is too simplistic to suggest that everyone can simply find another carer for their child. In cases like these, you will need to remind yourself of how your parent is, and try to not buy into it when they inevitably weaponise their help against you.

The silent treatment

The silent treatment is a destructive and powerful form of abuse and is one that is largely misunderstood. The silent treatment is not the same as going no-contact with someone, and it is not the same as being silent while you reflect and gather your thoughts. The silent treatment is the withdrawal of words, emotion and any love in an attempt to maintain control over someone. If you still have contact with your toxic parent, you may find the silent treatment being used seemingly without reason – or you may sometimes know exactly why. Either way, when it is deployed by someone that you are trying to maintain a relationship with, it can be overwhelming. They can go to great lengths with this, too, maintaining their silence with you while continuing to be happy and straightforward with others. I have also known of many instances where a toxic parent will encourage siblings to join in with the silence. If any siblings are of childhood age, they are often forced into joining in. When you experience the silent treatment, the best course of action is to not attempt to end the period of silence by trying to get them to engage. Instead, try your best to carry on as normal, showing as best you can that their silence has no control over you.

Leaving the door open

If you are in a no-contact or low-contact period, or a time during which you are not engaging with your toxic parent, they will always create the facade that they have left the door open for reconciliation. In some cases, their last contact can be a barrage of abuse and nastiness that then finishes by implying that their door is always open should you want to reconcile. This can again be incredibly confusing and is a way of manipulating the blame onto you. It is so they can convince themself, and anyone else around them, that they are trying to keep a relationship with you but that it is you who isn't willing to engage. You will likely see them spin this same narrative publicly, too – social media posts are a prime example, or you may hear from other people that they have been expressing how much they miss you and how unwilling you are to engage. Be clear in your mind and remember that this isn't you. Remember that you have spent a lifetime giving your parent every opportunity to have a proper relationship with you, and reconciliation is about both parties working together to mend the situation.

Social media parent

This is worth highlighting because I hear this from adult children of toxic parents all the time. You could be in the midst of a bitter episode with your parent where your last contact from them was venomous and you haven't heard from them since, and then you notice that on social media they have posted about their unwavering love for you or about how much they love being a parent. As with everything I have mentioned so far, this can be incredibly confusing. Although to some degree you may have become used to their behaviour, it can still have an impact. For this reason it is extremely common for adult children to block their parent's social media or, if that would create more problems than it solves, it can be worth muting them. Your toxic parent is consumed by how they are viewed by the people who haven't yet discovered their toxicity for what it is. This can also become part of the smear campaign, as explored in the previous chapter.

Sibling rivalry

On this journey in the coming chapters, you will learn about the different roles that you will have taken on growing up within the dysfunction of being raised by a toxic parent. If you have siblings, you may already be aware that you can sometimes have completely different experiences of your toxic parent. Your parent will have played an active role in making this the case, and will still play siblings against each other when it can benefit their current narrative and keep themself at the centre of the universe. If you have become the family member who is waking up most to the level of the toxicity that you have experienced, then you will be made the black sheep of the family. You will be seen by your parent – and anyone else unwilling to look at the abuse – as the crazy one. Stand strong in your truth and don't be drawn into trying to prove what you see to people who are only willing to discredit you for the sake of their own comfort. It is OK to be clear with siblings you still want to have a relationship with that one of the boundaries within that relationship is to not discuss your parent. More on boundaries in a moment.

The perfect grandparent

If you have become a parent yourself now, the relationship between your children and your toxic parent is one that will potentially raise some scenarios to navigate. Every situation is different and comes with its own set of complex circumstances. I wouldn't begrudge anyone who withholds contact with their children from their toxic parent entirely. If you feel it's the correct course of action, I firmly believe that you are well within your rights to do that. Why should the label of grandparent be a free pass for someone who has been abusive to have a relationship with your children now? I also understand that there are many other reasons why contact is needed. The most common thing I hear in this situation is that the toxic parent, if allowed contact with their grandkids, becomes the perfect loving grandparent for their grandchildren. Once again, this can cause deep confusion for you. It can make you feel like maybe your toxic parent was right all along, and you were the problem! This is, of course, not the case, and in some ways this is a continuation of the abuse, and even the smear campaign as outlined in the previous chapter. Boundaries are important in navigating what is right for you and your family in this instance. Knowing what is acceptable to you for the relationship to be tenable is really going to matter. Again, we will look at this in more detail later in this chapter.

Aging parent

This is arguably the most difficult situation to explore when it comes to your toxic parent. When they are aging or even becoming ill and the end of their life comes into focus, it can be a difficult time regardless of where you are at in terms of contact with them. I am not going to pretend there is a surefire way to navigate this, but I am also not going to ignore it either. I hear a range of different experiences of this circumstance. I hear many adult children who say they had gone no-contact, and that when their parent died it didn't change the way they felt at all. In many cases, they had done the large part of the grieving process when contact was cut. I have heard a number of people who had been no-contact for a long period of time and then when they heard that their parent had become ill, reconnected and supported them through their end of life, and who felt that this brought them some closure. And I have of course heard of many instances where it simply remains painful, messy and difficult to navigate. No instance is a reflection of you as a person; you are simply doing your best with the hand that you have been dealt. I do believe that by the time your journey with this book is over, you will feel more empowered to navigate the situation as best you can, and that is every reason to go on.

*

As I've said throughout, there is no right or wrong way to navigate all of the above scenarios. You may find that you recognise the scenarios clearly, or they will at least be similar to experiences that you have had. It may be that you felt like you were the only person on the planet who had to deal with something like this, or you may have even flittered between thinking you were losing your mind or that you were the problem. I want you to get clear on this before you go any further, so let me reiterate it: you are not crazy, you didn't cause any of this, and you are not alone.

JOURNAL PROMPTS

- Can you describe at least three regularly occurring scenarios that you experience at the hands of your toxic parent?
- For each scenario, describe how it makes you feel.
- Can you think of the best way to react in these scenarios?

Don't be too concerned if you struggled to adequately answer the third question. You are going to do some more work around this, and it is also something that will become clearer as you reclaim your power throughout this process.

BOUNDARIES

We will now look at some practical tips to help you feel more equipped to navigate the day-to-day life of being the adult child of a toxic parent. You will start by exploring the most important aspect of this: boundaries.

The process of finding and setting boundaries is often casually thrown around in the wellbeing space as if it's something that can happen at the click of a finger! This simply isn't the case. We are talking about toxic and abusive people, and the abuse doesn't just stop when boundaries are set. In many instances, the toxic parent will double down at the sight of a boundary. As a result, you will have a difficult relationship with boundaries. Even laying the most simple and obvious boundary can leave you feeling uneasy and out of your depth. At the hands of a toxic parent, you've had your boundaries constantly and consistently scuppered by the very people who should've been helping you set them. So, laying down boundaries has felt counterintuitive, and this is part of the reason you have found yourself so far into life without the ability to adequately set personal boundaries.

Once you have worked through this process and truly reclaimed your story, you will feel more empowered in laying boundaries, but it is worth getting as clear as you can around them and what they might look like. Remember, you are not a defenceless child anymore. You're a fully grown adult. You have lots of power at your disposal, from your intellect to your strength and your voice. It may not feel like this right now, but I can assure you that throughout this process you will see this much clearer. You do not need to make decisions in your life based on how it might impact the emotions of your parent, or anybody else dysfunctional from your childhood. Getting clear on your 'rights' is a great first step towards this.

Your rights are the fundamental rules or principles of what you will allow in your life. For example, in the context of the toxic parent relationship, you may wish to exercise your right to always be present when your children are around people who make you feel uncomfortable. Another might be the right to pick and choose the things that you like in your life, regardless of whether your parent dislikes or opposes them. Or even more simple, the right to express how you feel in any given moment.

Thinking specifically in the context of your relationship with your toxic parent, make a list of all of your rights. It is important to remember that these are your rights and nobody else's, so list everything that is a right for you, irrespective of how it might impact others.

Now you have the list of your rights in your life, I want you to think about a list of your core values. Your core values are the principles by which your life is led. I'm talking about the things that really matter to you in your life. Think about the reason that you continue to take steps forward in your life today: what keeps you doing that? Some examples could be your family, personal freedom or career, or even things like travel and adventure. Be bold here, these are YOUR core values, nobody else's. Go ahead and make a list of them.

Now that we have these two lists, reflect on them and notice what you've written down. These lists will help you to be clear in your mind about what you will and won't allow in your life. Anything that goes directly against the things in your lists is something that you should be seriously considering turning down or at least pushing back against. When your parent is behaving in any way that makes you feel uncomfortable and you're feeling confused and wondering whether you are overreacting, you can ask yourself two questions:

Does what's happening now violate any of my rights?

If I continue to allow what I am allowing, am I acting from my core values?

I would also encourage you to put these lists of rights and core values somewhere where you will see them regularly and be reminded of them, perhaps as your phone's screen saver, or keep copies of the lists up around your home to help you fully integrate them with who you are.

Now that you have some clarity on your boundaries I want to highlight a few more useful tips that can help you set better boundaries, before moving on to the next chapter and really diving into how to reclaim your story. I believe that all these tips will be of benefit to all adult children of toxic parents.

The first and sometimes hardest tip to take on board is to give up ever changing them. It is the great obsession of so many adult children with their toxic parent. In some cases, people don't even realise they are chasing this, it become subconscious, but it really is important to let go of it. For example, people can be well into their adulthood and still be pursuing a certain career in the hope that, in the end, it will make their parent love them the way they desire. Unfortunately, the chances of that ever happening are minimal. The truth is that you don't have the power to change anyone. Yes, in some instances you can influence others into change, but when it comes to toxic people the likelihood of change is almost zero. Not least because they have no desire to change themselves. Even if there is a small possibility of them ever changing, it is not something that you have any power in. Don't waste your life doing or being a certain version of yourself in the hope that it will change them.

Your life is your business. You are not obliged to tell or share any of it with anyone, especially not your toxic parent. They may still have a hold over you in this regard, guilt tripping you into sharing every detail of your life with them. You are an adult now and are entitled to your own life. If that wasn't in your list of rights, then go back and add it in! When things happen in your life, be it good news, bad news, happy news or indifferent news, you are allowed to choose who gets to share in that with you. When it comes to your toxic parent, there are two main reasons this is important. The first is simple and something that we have to some degree already explored: the fact that any information you share can and will be weaponised against you. You know this deep down, but sometimes your parent's hold over you wins out and you opt to tell them anyway. This is permission not to do that. The second reason is how they will make you feel as a result. If you have some difficult news, they are likely going to make it about them, thus making you feel worse. If you have some happy news, they will either do the same or otherwise mock you or do something to scupper your positive mood. So, be careful what you share and know it is OK to not share at all!

Know that it is OK to be blunt and cold with your toxic parent when needed. In fact, it's OK to be cold and blunt with anyone who isn't willing or able to validate your truth. Navigating your relationship with your toxic parent regardless of the level of contact that you have is hard enough, without forcing yourself to believe that you must act calmly and kindly in every instance. On this journey you will learn about some of the tendencies that you may have for people-pleasing and shrinking, but for now, just know that you can be whatever you need to be to best navigate each moment while protecting your wellbeing and emotional state. If that means feeling like you are cold, distant or even blunt in certain scenarios, that is completely acceptable. Protecting yourself is of higher importance than protecting the toxic parent who makes no attempt meet you halfway.

Something that you're going to need to understand, if you don't already, is that trying to reason or rationalise with your toxic parent is a complete waste of time and energy. You will never, ever win with them and they will never try to see things from your side, so engaging for that reason alone is pointless. It does go deeper than this, too. They will often try to bamboozle you with some of their interactions. The classic long, cryptic text message is a prime example of this, or if you have blocked their number, they will often send long letters. Reading any of these will typically lead to a desire to explain yourself and try to rationalise with them, and before you know it, you are pulled back into the toxicity and will find yourself embroiled in a tit-for-tat debate that you will never win. Your toxic parent is so capable of lying that they themself will believe what they are saying. Trying to bring logic to their distorted view of a situation never ends well and only causes you more stress and anxiety in the process. Where at all possible, try deciding not to engage and not getting pulled in by their attempts to do so.

You can also use closing statements to help with the times when you have to engage. A closing statement shuts down the conversations they will attempt to open. For example, they might remark how 'you haven't bothered to call round in ages', to which you can respond, 'I haven't called round in a while.' They are attempting to begin a discussion and expecting you to explain yourself. The moment you say anything to justify your actions they have something to come back on. Had you replied, 'I haven't, I've been busy,' they would have had the opportunity to come back and challenge your claim of being busy. The closing statement neither disagrees with them nor attempts to justify yourself.

As we explored in Chapter 1, your toxic parent firmly believes that they should be the centre of the universe and, as such, will still expect you to meet every one of their needs. If you haven't been able to push back on anything up until this point, then they will not even see you as an adult as such. They will still believe you are a child and that your duty is to serve them. This will be true particularly from an emotional standpoint. Despite never once being there for you and your emotions, they will still expect you to be emotionally available to them at the instant they feel it's necessary. Remember that you are not and have never been their parent, and you shouldn't feel guilty when you cannot be there for them at the drop of a hat. This is irrespective of how much they pull on your heartstrings and guilt-trip you into believing that not being there for them constitutes some kind of abandonment.

With all this in mind, put yourself first, always.

The reality is that a parent expecting you to put them and their feelings first shouldn't be a regularity. If you feel like this is a constant, then it's time to change that. You deserve to feel as if you, your emotions and your needs matter, and for that to happen you must put yourself first. The very thought of that may make you wince. It may feel uncomfortable, or it may even feel completely alien to you. Don't be too concerned if this is the case. By the end of this journey, I can assure you that putting yourself first will feel like the greatest gift.

JOURNAL PROMPTS

Before moving on to the next chapter and diving fully into the journey of reclaiming your story, reflect on what this chapter has brought up for you. Start by using the journal prompts below.

- What can you take from this chapter that will make you feel more equipped in managing life as an adult child of a toxic parent?
- How clear are you on your boundaries, and how can you make sure you keep your rights and core values in mind?
- What is one major and impactful commitment that you can make to the management of life with a toxic parent?

Breathwork

Once you have completed the journal prompts, it is time to deepen your practice with conscious connected breathing. The breathwork here will again help you gain an understanding of how it's done before we begin the full conscious connected practice in the coming chapters. Use the QR code below to learn about the breathwork.

3. HEALING IN COMMUNITY

The things that you believe keep you alone in this world will in fact connect you to more people than you could ever imagine.

The previous chapter may have been a complete revelation, or it could have simply confirmed what you already knew deep down. Either way, it can feel desperately lonely. Most people assume that loneliness is solely about how many people they have in their life, but it is also driven by how much of themselves they are willing or able to share with others. Much of what you will have explored in Chapter 1 concerns thoughts and feelings you may not have been able to openly explore with anyone. Every single feeling you have that you are unable to publicly share is a part of yourself that feels alone. Whether it is because there is nobody to fully witness it, because you have been actively running away from the pain, or because you simply haven't found the words for it, you will have experienced loneliness. Your secrets have kept you sick because you have been left alone with them. Having a toxic parent can mean that your whole childhood is a secret. If you reflect on how everyone is a product of their childhood, it's inevitable that loneliness will have played a part in your life.

> YOU DO NOT DESERVE TO BE COMPLETELY ALONE IN THIS LIFE. THIS WAS NEVER YOUR FAULT.

DISMANTLING YOUR FORTRESS

In a desperate act of self-protection, you have spent a lifetime building a fortress around yourself in order to feel safe. So many big and powerful feelings have had to stay hidden, and that vulnerable and delicate part of yourself that absorbed all the pain of having a toxic parent needed protecting. So, you built walls. You stayed emotionally closed off in a host of different ways. You may have become the joker, the carer or even the quiet one, but at some level you will have worked hard to maintain your protective walls. Irrespective of the size of your social circle, you found a way to build walls. In this chapter we are going to gently dismantle some of the fortresses you have built around yourself, in order to understand the importance of true community as the antidote to some of your loneliness. As scary as it may feel, a vital part of your journey will involve beginning to gently explore allowing people in.

What comes up for you when you reflect on your own loneliness?

How connected do you feel to the people in your life?

How much of yourself is there that nobody knows about, and can you explore what these parts of yourself are?

Don't worry if these questions fail to stir much up for you. Keep them in your mind as you read on, seeing whether they evoke more insight as you go. I want to share with you my experience of loneliness, and the devastating impact that it can have.

Loneliness was something I experienced deeply. When I was 24, I got sober from alcohol and drugs. Before then, I couldn't have articulated that I was lonely, but it quickly became inescapable as I entered recovery. I did what I had always done: I created a version of myself that wasn't actually me; it was just another character I could become. This time it was 'the sober guy'. This was my attempt at keeping my fortress strong. Rather than sharing my struggle with people, I found a new way to hide it.

I have always managed to maintain a large social circle. Even in my darkest drinking days, I was still well liked by a lot of people, but my behaviour was a performance, and it was nearly always at the expense of my true self. I thought giving up alcohol would make my problems go away, but in truth it left me with them. All the thoughts and feelings that I had always used alcohol to escape from came back in floods, and I simply could not handle it. I was 24 and had never once spoken honestly about how I felt or what I had experienced, so I didn't even know where to begin. I couldn't communicate what I was feeling with anyone. It was something that I had never done before. I was too used to being what I thought people wanted. When I decided to give up alcohol, I no longer had anything to numb the pain and I just couldn't cope.

My attempts at protecting myself and coping were the very things that kept me alone. How many of your coping mechanisms are keeping you alone? Your experience may not be as extreme as the one I am sharing but, reflecting on the three questions I posed, are there any similarities?

I wasn't very far into my sober journey when I seriously planned to end my life. It had taken me 12 years to drink myself almost to death but only 9 months to nearly 'sober' myself to death. I truly believed that the best thing for me and everyone in my life would be to end it all. Despite having lots of people around me, I felt like I was going to die alone, hiding in plain sight. At the moment that I planned on leaving this world, nobody on the planet knew who I really was or what I was experiencing. Everyone thought I was in the best place I'd ever been. I had found sobriety and was declaring that I had seen the light. But the truth was that things were darker than they had ever been. Ending my life felt like a very honest, noble and selfless decision. It felt like the best thing for me and the best thing for everyone who knew me, too. That is where my thinking took me, and, because I wouldn't share anything with anyone, nobody was ever going to tell me any different. Fortunately, that plan was broken by a weekend with my children that changed everything. As I knew I was going to die, the past had become irrelevant and the future non-existent, and for the first time ever in my life I was present with my children, and this is what changed my mind.

I remember cuddling my daughter and feeling it in a way I had never experienced. I saw my son go down a slide and look back at me to check I was watching. It was the first time in my life that I had ever been truly present for those moments. It was this connection that saved my life; I was forced into presence and could no longer hide behind the thoughts and feelings that had guarded me my entire life.

The Monday following that weekend was the first time I ever sat within a community of people and spoke my truth. I was going to Alcoholics Anonymous at the time, or AA, as it is commonly known. This is a fellowship of people who work through a programme and go to regular group meetings. They work a bit like group therapy, but are peer-to-peer led. Those groups had been a safe haven for me but were still not somewhere I was completely honest. That day was different, though. I sat in a room full of people and poured out my gut-wrenching truth about how much I hated life. It was my first time ever doing this and, as a result, the first time I could remember feeling truly connected to others without the use of a mind-altering substance.

I finally felt like I was part of something; I felt seen and alive. Most importantly, I realised that everything I had felt kept me alone in this world was actually connecting me with more people than I could have ever imagined. In those moments, shame cannot survive.

I understand as deeply as anyone the urge to keep those walls up and to keep people out. I cannot deny the comfortable lure of staying in one's fortress, but my experience has shown me in the clearest way that, without true connection, you can't survive in your fortress alone.

This is why community can become the cornerstone of your healing journey. Not just because you will be regularly witnessed, but also because you will be witnessing others who are on a similar journey. I am not suggesting you must completely dismantle your fortress, but can you begin to let people in? There are people ahead of you, people behind you, and people going through the exact same thing. Witnessing them is often the door to the biggest breakthroughs. In witnessing others, you will witness yourself.

The importance of sharing

Opening up is hard. Beginning to talk about thoughts, feelings and experiences you have spent a lifetime hiding and protecting is not easy. Regular sharing will play a huge role in supporting that. This is slightly different to just talking. Sharing is about revealing parts of yourself in a way that allows you to be witnessed, and there is a huge amount of healing in that alone. This goes against everything you were taught growing up in a toxic environment, where you learned to hide large parts of who and what you truly are. A fundamental part of any healing journey will include access to regular spaces in your life to share. All those thoughts that you have whizzing and rumbling around your head are best sorted through by sharing and allowing others to hear them.

Having someone witness you on your own level is something that goes much deeper than just listening. Can you recall a time when you talked to someone and came away thinking, *Wow, I've just shared my entire experience with that person, and I have no idea why.* Well, it is because they made you feel truly heard; they witnessed you. True listening goes beyond words. It is about feeling and then leaning in to that feeling to really sit with someone. You step into their darkness not to fix, not to change, but just to sit for a while so that they might feel seen and heard. That is where witnessing truly happens.

Being witnessed in this way throughout childhood is a fundamental thing that is lacking in the dysfunction created by the toxic parent outlined in the previous chapters. It is going to feel alien to you, and leaning in to it may feel uncomfortable. It is OK to take baby steps towards becoming open to this.

When was the last time you were truly witnessed? Think about this and again reflect on the three questions posed at the beginning of this chapter. How much are you hiding? This isn't about shouting about your story to anyone who will listen, but, if you were to think of the three closest people in your life today, how much of your truth have you shared with them?

Perhaps you have spoken in some detail about your experiences with those closest to you, but have you truly been able to open up? Have you been able to share some of the ways those experiences made you feel so that you can be witnessed?

It makes sense that you may not have done this with even the closest people to you, because growing up with a toxic parent means you weren't supported through your struggles. In Chapter 1 we looked at how you were instead made to feel like those struggles made you an annoyance and even unlovable. You pushed those feelings down into your body and remained completely alone with them. It was your only way to stay safe, and it meant building a protective fort around yourself. Your attempts to make yourself lovable became the very thing that kept you alone in this world.

You were taught to abandon yourself instead of having your innate value loved and nurtured. To show your emotion was to create conflict, as your toxic parent may have seen your emotional expression in direct opposition to their feelings. You are terrified by the thought that in order to express your true needs you would create conflict. If you have ever expressed or spoken about your needs with someone in your life who cares about you, did you apologise after, as if it were wrong of you to burden them with your feelings? It may even be that you don't remember ever expressing your needs in this way. This was your reality when you were creating your sense of self in relation to how others would love you. So, today you tend to approach your relationships with the intention of meeting all the other person's needs, even at the expense of yourself and your own needs. You will create whole new belief patterns in the moment if it means making yourself more likeable or lovable to the person you are interacting with. You hide your true feelings from people, and you do it in a range of different ways. You often know you are doing it, too, and that's probably the worst part. The people that could genuinely witness you in your life today are the people you are least likely to share with! Again, in the context of what we discussed in Chapter 1, this makes perfect sense. Your toxic parent taught you that your needs and emotions were a burden and so you have become conditioned to keep them from the people you care about.

I encourage you to now make a mental list of the three closest people in your life and practise trying to let them in. This might feel difficult or forced at first, but it is something that is worth the discomfort. There may be one of those three names jumping out at you most and it is OK to start with them. Can you open up and let them know you have embarked on this journey? Sharing doesn't have to begin with an intense face-to-face conversation. Maybe you could write an email or a letter or send a voice note? I appreciate this may feel daunting and a part of the process you would rather skip, but really try and give it a go. You might start with something like:

'I am not looking for solutions, answers or even words of reflection, but I am going on a personal journey of healing and I want to get better at sharing more of my vulnerable truth with you . . .'

You could then follow this with an outline of one or some of your experiences. Try to explore their impact on you and how you have felt and acted as a result. You might say something like:

'As a result, I have often felt like I am worthless and so pushed you away.'

How are you feeling at the prospect of this? The very thought of it could be making you cringe. This is a sure sign that you should try it. Why would sharing your truth with the people you care most about make you cringe or despair? If you are beginning to push back against the loneliness created by your parent's toxicity, then it is important to lean in to these uncomfortable moments.

As a note for some readers, you may have one person (or more) in your list of three closest people who doesn't make you feel safe enough to do this exercise with, for reasons that are not linked to your own struggle with it. I am pointing to people in your life who may be toxic or abusive themselves. I ask that you trust your intuition as much as you can on this one. If this is the case, then you do not need to share any of the above with those people. There is a lesson here for everyone too. We exist in a world that sometimes wants to believe that healing means being completely open all the time with everyone. I don't believe this to be the case at all, and though I encourage you to work on sharing your secrets with those closest to you, I must stress that you only do so with people you trust.

Building your community

Finding and building a safe and trusting community is so important, especially in today's world. It can be easy to fall into the isolation trap. It doesn't have to be a huge network, but finding your people really matters. You will need to practise being the version of yourself that you are becoming. As you do this, you will need people around you that you trust and feel safe with.

Everyone needs a home, somewhere you can walk through the door and know that it is safe to drop the act and be completely who you are in that moment, with no need to self-organise. Metaphorically speaking, your community can become this for you. Being witnessed in a completely non-judgemental way by others can begin to feel like being held. Some of the weight is carried by others and your loneliness begins to dissipate.

Don't panic if the thought feels overwhelming or unreachable from where you are right now; you can take baby steps. It may not come naturally to you at first, in fact it might be incredibly uncomfortable, but it is completely possible. I appreciate you may start this work alone because that's all you can muster, or maybe it's all you have. But I want to encourage you to eventually find a sense of community. As you continue the steps in this book, you will also become more empowered and will grow your community organically. However, there are steps I encourage you to take that will push you out of your comfort zone. As well as leaning in to the close relationships in your life today (in the ways that you already have in this chapter), I am going to outline how you can use this journey to begin to widen your community too.

HOW TO EXPAND YOUR COMMUNITY FOR HEALING

Address current community

Away from your toxic parent and family dysfunction, think about friends that are or have been in your life. Are there friendships that have fallen away but could be rebuilt? What about relationships that are strong but in which you are still hiding for reasons mentioned above? As we have explored, it's in our closest relationships that we tend to hide the most. Maybe there are some relationships in your life that have become more of a drain and no longer serve you? Having explored loneliness in more detail, be sure to take some time to nurture what is there already.

Paired work

You could go through the work in this book with someone else who may also need it. Set some accountability dates that you will complete certain sections by, and then share your experiences and what comes up, witnessing each other in the process! This will help you lean in to sharing and building trust, but will also help to ensure you complete the work and exercises needed. If you feel you don't know anyone who would want to work through this book, perhaps find someone who might be willing to listen to and witness your experience.

Online sharing

When you feel safe enough, perhaps you could start by sharing some things online? Anonymity can be helpful in the beginning, giving you the courage to share more openly. There are so many different types of community that can be found online. You could even start an account with the sole purpose of sharing your journey.

You have discovered the level of toxicity that you have endured, and you are already beginning to step into your power. If you haven't already, then you may find yourself becoming ostracised from your family as you begin to see things for what they are. This is known as becoming the black sheep of the family. We explored some of the reasoning for this in Chapter 1. When people are too afraid to clearly see the truth of the toxicity, they will shun the person speaking that truth. If you are the only one in the family who is doing this, then you may remain the only black sheep, not just in the eyes of the toxic parent but in the eyes of everyone within the family who is unaware or unable to look directly at the dysfunction. This can be a lonely place and it may even create distance between you and good people within your family.

If for no other reason, it is important to avoid isolating yourself, and you can counter this by starting to find and be with your people. You will need them, and you will need them to understand and metaphorically hold your hand while you navigate a situation you never signed up for. You may also find that community can further dispel the myth that you only get one mum and dad. Community can bring with it a number of mother and father figures who can have a hugely positive impact on your life, and you can have as many mothers and fathers as you need. A good job too, because along the journey people may evolve in and out of being parental figures in your life. Some people will actively play more than one role. And ultimately, you will outgrow some people altogether – a painful reality of the healing journey.

JOURNAL PROMPTS

Before moving on to the next chapter, let's revisit the questions from the beginning of this chapter more closely. I have added some more, too.

- What comes up for you when you reflect on your own loneliness?
- How connected do you feel to the people in your life?
- How much of yourself is there that nobody knows about, and can you explore what these parts of yourself are?
- How do you feel at the thought of possibly sharing this with someone close to you?
- What type of connection are you yearning for?

Have your answers to the first three questions shifted since doing some of the exercises outlined in this chapter? Having begun to further connect with the people close to you, you may find yourself wanting to deepen those relationships and to create more space in your life for those moments of genuine connection. If this is the case, then that is great and I would encourage you to continue to create more of those moments throughout the process of this work.

It may also be the case that, after opening yourself up to deeper connections, you experienced an urge to rebuild your fortress that felt even stronger than it was previously. This is normal, and I don't want to push back against that too hard because it is your safety mechanism and there are a number of reasons this may have happened. It could be that the person you shared with did not respond in a way that made you feel safe. It could be that it was an overwhelming experience for you, and you need plenty of time to process and rest before thinking about sharing again. Or it could simply be your old protective habits taking hold. All of these reasons make complete sense. In this instance, it's OK to take a lot more time for further reflection before diving back in and opening yourself up again.

Breathwork

Remember, this isn't a race or something that you need to become an expert in; rather, it's about taking the time to stretch as far out of your comfort zone as you can while learning from your reactions. Breathwork is a great way to do this. Before jumping into the next chapter, it is time for another breathwork session. After the breathing sessions in Chapters 1 and 2, you should now have an understanding of the breathing pattern you'll use at the end of each chapter. You will now breathe and reflect on the experiences of this chapter while also turning towards the next part of the work.

4.
BODY FIRST

How often do you try to convince yourself that you are OK, while knowing all the while that you don't believe yourself?

How often do you sense that you have lots of feelings in your body that you can't describe without sounding crazy?

How often do you get a strong feeling in your body about something that you ignore, and the instinct turns out to be correct?

Before reading on, take some time now to note down any sensations that you feel in your body. What you write doesn't have to make sense to anyone else and it doesn't have to feel like you are using 'correct' terminology. I just want you to note down what you feel. If I were to do this myself, I might write:

There is a slightly dull ache across the lower part of my back. I can feel a slight fizziness in my tummy, and I have some butterflies in my chest – not big ones, but I can feel them. My shoulders feel hunched and tight.

The small act of doing this can show a lot about what you are feeling. We often completely ignore our bodies in attempts to think or rationalise our way out of what we are feeling. Gaining even a surface-level understanding of your nervous system can help empower you to feel more equipped in navigating your day-to-day flow of emotions. Doing this is the opposite to so much of what is taught in the wellness space, where we are often encouraged to ignore or not believe our thoughts. To help you with the reflective work that will follow in the coming chapters, I am going to help you to start thinking in a 'body first' way.

WHAT IS THE BODY FIRST APPROACH?

So much of what is taught when it comes to navigating emotions deals only with thought. We are told that we are not our thoughts, or to ignore them or just to reframe them. This is all well and good and can sometimes bring some temporary relief, but that is mostly because it keeps you in a thought cycle and ignores your body. Thinking in a body first way is about starting at your body and becoming curious about what it is trying to tell you. In doing so, you can learn to move through emotions. As a result, your thoughts will change.

Take what you have noted at the beginning of this chapter on what you're feeling in your body and become curious about the clues your body may be giving you. In my example I finished by saying that my shoulders felt 'hunched and tight'. Why might that be? I'm passionate about what I'm writing and have a strong desire to communicate my thoughts adequately, and my tight shoulders point to some tension in that. That tension makes sense, but I want to relax into this as much as possible. Allowing my shoulders to drop, giving them some movement and a couple of deep breaths, instantly helps to release some of that tension. My thoughts move from a slightly tense 'I have to do this well' to a more relaxed 'I've got this!' This simple example of a body first approach is something you can move towards.

Growing up with a toxic parent, you were forced to close off from your emotions so that you could fall in line with doing and being what your parent needed. I am thinking particularly about not allowing you to explore your emotions and the gaslighting that we explored in detail in Chapter 1, and how this has left you unable to trust what your body tells you.

The struggle of ignoring your body is something further compounded by societal beliefs in general. In my experience, people in Western culture tend to be at least slightly emotionally avoidant.

My dad died when I was young. At his funeral I remember people encouraging me to be brave. Some told me to be brave for my mum. They were literally telling a nine-year-old boy not to cry at his dad's funeral because his mum had enough on her plate! It's not that they were in any way ill-intentioned, but the reality of what they were telling me was to not burden my mum with how I was feeling. That might make you feel uncomfortable, but it is a blunt and honest account of what they were saying. Think about what is truly meant when we tell someone to be brave. What we actually mean is: 'I don't think I can deal with the emotion that I know you need to express right now, so

I am going to tell you to be brave, to hold it in and allow me to feel more comfortable.' It comes from a place of fear. People are terrified of emotions. Anyone who can 'hold it together' in times of sadness is glorified and celebrated for staying in a comfortable state of avoidance.

Avoidance of emotions is something that will have started as result of your toxic parent's dysfunction, and you will have experienced it most of your life. You can probably relate to people celebrating your recital of a traumatic incident like it was nothing. Rarely does someone offer what you truly lack: people who can witness you fully in your experience while allowing whatever emotion is evoked in you to come through. Instead, you are forced to stuff it back into a nicely wrapped box while pretending it wasn't that bad. Everyone does this, and nobody seems capable of simply acknowledging that some things we go through are bloody awful and it is OK to feel bloody awful as a result.

Moving towards a body first approach means having a basic understanding of your nervous system. This is not something most of us are ever introduced to growing up. Instead, we are taught to only ever rationalise our thoughts and, if the feelings don't add up, they must simply be ignored. As a result, it is no wonder that so many people reach adulthood with a continued and strong desire to numb out or escape. It is time to undo some of this conditioning and get back to being completely in tune with your body. We will do this by reflecting on the importance of the nervous system.

THE NERVOUS SYSTEM AND ITS THREE STATES

The nervous system is your body's command centre, sending messages back and forth between your brain and your body. It is an integral part of how you live your life, and yet most people are completely unaware of it. Instead, we are often taught that the way we feel is all in our heads, completely disregarding the way our bodies feel. Growing up with a toxic parent will have left you not trusting your feelings, and I want to help you regain that trust.

Your experience of your nervous system can be split down into three states: your relaxed state, your stressed state and your survival state. Your relaxed state is the state you ought to be in most often. The relaxed state should be accessible whenever you are alone at home relaxing, or in the company of people you care about. It is where you feel most comfortable. You enter your stressed state whenever there is a perceived threat or some pressure. Typical examples would be working to a tight deadline, driving on a busy road, or perhaps even on the school run. At the right levels it can make you alert and help keep you motivated for the task at hand. The survival state, however, is somewhere you wouldn't often find yourself. Typically, this would be a state reserved for a prolonged period of grief, or when you have reached an emotional burnout when you have faced overwhelming or chronic levels of stress.

Even with these short definitions, it is easy to see how growing up with a toxic parent in the environment that you did would have an impact on how you move through these states.

Reflect on these three questions, and then explore the outline of each state below in some more detail.

JOURNAL PROMPTS

- How often do you think you are in the relaxed state?
- How easily do you think you can move from the stressed state to the relaxed state?
- How strongly does the survival state resonate with you?

Relaxed state

Your relaxed state is meant to be your default state, the state that you should be able to return to whenever you want to decompress. In your relaxed state the world feels like a much safer place. You have a childlike curiosity to explore the world and what's in it. Co-regulation feels natural. This means that you can support others through emotions as well as feel supported through your own. Giving support also feels like something you want to do, as compassion is the starting place of how you see the people around you. Being present doesn't feel like a chore, and there is a sense of hope for the future.

In an ideal world, you would be able to create clear pathways to access this state when you're ready and need to. But most people aren't even aware they need to, let alone possess a way of getting there. Your natural level of sensitivity and the level of dysfunction you experienced in your formative years will correspond to how difficult you find this state to access and be in. With childhood dysfunction, you learned and in many cases were taught that the world was a scary place. This may have been through the arguments you saw between the adults in your life, or through the interactions you had with them. A toxic parent doesn't like curiosity – it can make them feel exposed and means that they have to explain their actions. They will have used a lot of the tactics we have previously explored to sabotage all the ingredients you needed to be in your relaxed state.

For children of toxic parents, this state can be extremely hard to access for any desired length of time. In Chapter 1 I talked about walking on eggshells. This meant that any time there was a calm moment you were fearful of the next outburst or accusation, and so it was the calm itself that pushed you back out of this state. For this very reason, you may find the breathing techniques that are designed to be calming actually induce anxiety for you.

This means that, as an adult, you will spend more time in one of the other states and may find it extremely difficult to move into this one.

Stressed state

You will find yourself here when you need to get things done or when your nervous system senses a threat. It comes with a sense of unease and danger. You are quick to anger or to feel anxious and overwhelmed, often unable to assign these feelings to anything in particular and with nowhere to focus the resulting energy. You are hypervigilant, and you find it extremely difficult to switch off. You are on edge and looking for signs of danger and often misread those signs. For example, you will find yourself repeatedly asking the people around you whether they are

OK or if you have upset them in some way. You are in a state of disconnection with connection, feeling uncomfortable and unattractive.

This is a state that, from day to day, we do need. It motivates you to get things done and can get you moving with the things that matter. When you are in danger of any kind, being stressed will motivate you to do what's needed. But you don't want to be here all of the time, particularly for no real reason. It is likely that when you are in this state, you don't know how to move out of it.

You probably spent a lot of time in this state as a child. If you are constantly looking for and expecting danger, you are much easier to control. The toxic parent will actively and intuitively use this to their advantage, but it will also happen subconsciously within dysfunctional environments. In Chapter 1 you learned how a toxic parent only gives space to their own emotions, and never to yours. This will mean that you were lacking in someone to help you navigate the natural and difficult emotions that come with life. As a child, how often did an adult sit you on their knee during difficult moments with big emotions, and just be with you in that experience? You likely learned very early on to not even go to your parent with your difficult feelings. If you're not sure about this, think of the earliest memory you have of an emotional struggle and then think about which parent you took that struggle to. Many of you will answer that you didn't take it to a parent, and this is because, for many of the reasons outlined in Chapter 1, you learned not to.

Co-regulation, the act of having someone calmly move with you through difficult and stressful experiences, was off the cards.

As result, you never learned to self-regulate. This means that, as an adult, you push through moments of stress or heightened emotion. Rather than naturally soothing yourself through difficult times, you push all feelings down into your body while convincing yourself and those around you that you are OK. Those feelings don't go away; they seep into your life in different ways. For example, after a stressful day at work, you may end up being grumpy or even nasty with your partner, children or yourself.

Survival state

Have you ever felt like you are watching life happen from behind a screen? Like you're there, taking part, but not quite connected? This is the survival state, the less recognised of the three states mentioned and arguably the most problematic. Here you will find yourself in conservation mode, looking only to survive. You will feel numb and your thoughts will be foggy. A sense of loneliness is ever present and can feel like abandonment. You feel hopeless and the idea of a safe space is unimaginable.

You will look for ways to feel something – anything – in this state. This may take the form of risky or irrational behaviour to counter the numbness. Binging and addictive-type behaviours are also common as you look for comfort in your loneliness. It is an incredibly confusing place for you and the people who care about you. Your actions can appear more self-destructive than survival.

This is a protective state, though. You will go here when your experience is too overwhelming. Nearly all the traits of a toxic parent that we have discussed will have had the power to take you here as a child. These traits will have been incredibly overwhelming, and your stressed state will have led to more problems at the hands of your parent. So, your nervous system will have done its job and tuned you out. This makes sense, and what an amazing survival technique to develop. The issue is that you still go there a lot as an adult and, as with your stressed state, you have no idea that you're doing it or how to address it. When the nervous system senses similar situations to the ones that put you in a survival state when you were a child, it does the same for you now. Couple this with never being taught how to adequately soothe yourself, and you likely find you're unknowingly here a lot. You can tell looking back when you have been in this state as you will have been so lacking in presence that you won't be able to recall whole conversations and experiences.

Having now explored each state in more detail, let's revisit the questions I posed before.

How often do you think you are in the relaxed state?

How easily do you think you can move from the stressed state to the relaxed sate?

How strongly does the survival state resonate with you?

You will likely realise that the relaxed state is a state you find hard to reach. Growing up in dysfunction means that as a child, the relaxed state was not one that was often found in the home.

When it comes to the survival state, rather than it being the state that you sparingly visit (as I originally alluded to), it is somewhere that you may find you often get stuck in. Growing up in a difficult and dysfunctional environment means that you were never supported in soothing yourself through difficult emotions. As we explored in detail in Chapter 1, most of your emotions were actively worked against and forced back down into your body with no way of being released. If you found yourself in the stressed state as a child, it will have become increasingly difficult to morph into the version of yourself that you felt was acceptable to your parent, and so rather than find ways to come back into your relaxed state your only real option was to go into survival state. This can be a difficult and even upsetting discovery, but I want you to also try seeing it in a positive light, too. Your experiences in so many instances as a child were simply too painful to comprehend, and yet you found a way through. This is something to be proud of. Unfortunately, your body and your nervous system are still reacting to the world from that place. This isn't something that you can simply think your way out of. You need to keep the connection with your body as much as you can.

Can you think of many times when your parent would help you work through your tears? When they would sit with you, cuddle you and let you cry it out while helping you remember things would be OK? If the answer is very few or even never, then it makes sense that your connection with your body is one that has been severed over time. Being in your body will have been a scary place. This is why I struggle with the term 'mental health'. We are not talking about an experience that you went through in your mind, we are talking about a very physical and deep full-body experience.

Picture a child of around four or five years old for a moment. If you have children of your own or any that you are close to then picture them. Imagine, for a moment, their innocence, their childlike wonder and curiosity. Now gently imagine that this child has come to you upset. See their eyes for a moment; they're confused, struggling. Now, imagine they are scared of your reaction, and they are trying to hide their feelings from you.

How do you feel reflecting on that?

Where in your body was most activated during the reflection, and what sensations arose?

Now, think about what will have been going on in the child's body, and the effort they will have had to put in just to get by.

Take a moment here. Though this may seem like a very simple reflection, it is a profound one. Even writing it myself, I noticed how I held my breath. Try taking one deep breath in through your nose, and out through your nose. Repeat this breath pattern five times. Each time that you do, elongate both the inhale and the exhale until, on the fifth round, you're on the edge of breathing in too slowly.

Notice the effect this short breathing pattern has on your body. It may not bring you back to an entirely tranquil state, especially when you have a nervous system that has been affected in the way we have described, but it does at least put a bend in the road when it feels like you're losing control of your body's reaction.

Thinking again about the child that you visualised, bring your thoughts now to your own experience. Can you start to see the long-lasting impact of your experiences growing up, and how hard you must have worked to navigate your life up to this stage? Can you perceive the stress your body will have been under, just to get by? Simply trying to rationalise your experience is often the only way you would try to soothe yourself and bring yourself back to your relaxed state. This might have been by always finding the silver lining, reflecting on how your situation really could be a lot worse, or by creating excuses for why your parent was and is the way that they are. It is not that none of these things has any relevance and can't be useful in some way, but, when they come only at the expense of how you truly feel, it becomes problematic as your body is working so hard with all the emotions it has to absorb as a result.

This is why so many self-development practices feel like they finish at a dead end for you. In the end, they're just another way to rationalise your way out of feeling your truth. Growing up with a toxic parent, you will have had no shortage of people helping you navigate back to that silver lining in order to avoid the discomfort. What you have truly lacked is someone to come and be with you in those difficult emotions. Most people over-rationalise and jump straight to positivity or fixing mode, completely ignoring the body in the process. We can all be guilty of doing this. Instead of really listening to someone's experience, we jump straight to fixing, which smothers their feelings in the process. It is the most common sentence I hear from people justifying their need to fix others: that they just want people to be OK. Though there is some truth in these claims, I believe something else is at play here.

Think about a time when someone you cared about came to you with a really difficult struggle. Can you think of any other reason that you might jump directly to offering solutions or trying to fix the issue for them? Could the way the situation made you feel be one of the things that drove your need to fix?

I reached a conclusion on this myself when reflecting on my strong desire to fix. I noticed that when people I particularly cared about came to me with some kind of struggle, I would take on the role of fixer. A perfect example of this would be how I interact with my own children. When they come to me with a struggle, the pull to smother the situation with positivity is almost overpowering. I too used to tell myself that it was just a reflection of how much I love them and how much I want them to be OK – which is of course all true. But with more reflection, I realised what was truly going on. When my children brought me their struggles I couldn't handle the way it made me feel, and so the positivity wasn't even about them – it was about me and my desire to escape the difficult resulting emotions.

What most people who are struggling really want and need is to feel seen and witnessed in what they are experiencing. They want for you to step into their darkness and sit for a while so they might feel heard. They need you to metaphorically hold their hand so that they don't have to feel alone in that experience. Of course, people need to hear that things are going to be OK, but positivity at the expense of validation is useless.

This further highlights what I alluded to when exploring

the stressed state: most people suppress their emotions in the hope they will disappear, only for those emotions to come out of them sideways. This usually means hurting those close you. Maybe you lash out at a loved one? Perhaps you go into yourself and withdraw from communication? Or maybe you escape into your vice? You likely also gaslight yourself, telling yourself you are overreacting to situations, when your reactions are entirely justified. This repeats the patterns that played out in the home you grew up in. Instead of looking at the wider picture and being curious about why you may feel that way, you are encouraged to find a reason why you shouldn't feel like this. You're made to think that the way you feel is wrong, and something that needs to be fixed.

Being in your body and experiencing your emotions is hard enough. Add to this a lack of support in soothing yourself growing up, and it is easy to see why you may get caught escaping your reality and ignoring your nervous system altogether. The common belief is that if someone is struggling with the way they feel, then the solution is to make them feel better. This is wrong. When someone is struggling with how they feel, they need people to help them be better at feeling. They need to know they are safe to be in their feelings and to release them, to be held and free from judgement.

The good news is you can bring all of this together and start to retrain yourself to not only better understand your nervous system but feel better equipped in each state. Let's take a deeper look at the three states: the relaxed state, the stressed state and the survival state. In the next exercise, I want you to explore how it feels to be in each. Take some time in a safe and comfortable space to work through them one at a time. When reflecting on each state, lean in to the feeling of being in the state but be careful not to go there fully. Around 15 per cent of the feeling will be enough, but try for less if that feels safer.

EXERCISE: EXPLORING YOUR THREE STATES

Start by thinking about the survival state and allowing yourself to lean in. Can you summarise what this feels like for you in a few sentences? How often are you in the survival state? Where in your body is most activated when in this state? Now complete the following exercise by answering the questions in bold. I've left my own answers in italics to help get you started.

When I am in the survival state my life seems . . .

Difficult, heavy, distant and hazy.

When I am in the survival state my relationships are . . .

Fractured, distant and almost non-existent.

In the survival state what I need most is . . .

Something to help me feel in my body in a healthy way.

Once you have explored the survival state, move now to the stressed state. Can you summarise what it feels like here? How often are you in this state, and where in your body is most activated? Then, complete the three sentences once again:

When I am in the stressed state my life seems . . .

When I am in the stressed state my relationships are . . .

In the stressed state what I need most is . . .

Finally, and hopefully more pleasant to explore, is the relaxed state. This is the state that should be regularly accessible to us. How often are you in this state, and where in your body does it show up most? Finally, complete the three sentences again.

When I am in the relaxed state my life seems . . .

When I am in the relaxed state my relationships are . . .

In the relaxed state what I need most is . . .

Having fully reflected on all three states in more detail alongside the previous reflections, you can now bring some more awareness whenever you are in any of the states in your day-to-day life. However, knowledge itself is not enough. This is where building a relationship with your breath can be the tool to bring more power back into your life. Through the introductions to breathwork at the end of the previous chapters, you have already begun that journey. I now want to go into a bit more detail about the benefits of this breathwork, and why I believe it to be so important.

BREATHING INTO YOUR BODY

Breathing into your body is about using the power of your breath to reconnect your mind with your body. Being in your body is vital if you are to truly feel all the emotions that you have been forced to avoid throughout most of your life. When you are fully in your body you cannot avoid your emotions, and so you spend a lot of time in your head. Thinking, rationalising and busy internal dialogues are all ways of staying in our heads in order to avoid being in our bodies and feeling our emotions. Breathing and building a relationship with how you breathe can be exactly what you need in order to come back into your body.

I have been an expert at not being in my body and retreating into my head in this way. It is still my number-one way of avoiding how I feel. It is why just talking only gets me so far. I can explain exactly how I know I am supposed to feel in any given situation, without ever actually having to feel it. This isn't something I set out to do. In fact, I actively push back against it, but I find it can still happen. It means that, in most settings, simply talking about how I feel leaves me wanting. It is like my brain kicks in, takes over and doesn't let me connect to my body in the way I truly need. I feel emotions very deeply and so being with them can feel incredibly uncomfortable. Couple this with a lack of support to soothe myself through these emotions in my childhood, and I can see why my brain would want this protective strategy for me.

For me, though, it goes a step further than that simple protective strategy. When I think about the times that I have engaged in different one-on-one therapies, I become a good patient. People-pleasing is something that you will explore in more detail in the next chapter but my own people-pleasing tendencies take over in these instances. Instead of checking in with myself and exploring the answers to the therapist or counsellor's questions, I figure out why they have asked them, and then construct the perfect answer. By this I mean the perfect answer for them, not me. At some level, I know that I am going to have to avoid the emotion to protect myself, but I become concerned about letting the therapist down too. I begin answering in the way I know I should in order to make sure they feel like the session is going well, while simultaneously dodging ever being in my body and feeling anything. So much of the questions asked don't touch me, let alone have a lasting impact. By the end of the session the therapist leaves feeling like there's been a major breakthrough, and all I get is the badge of honour of being the perfect patient. When you couple strong people-pleasing tendencies with a strong need or desire to avoid your emotions, simply talking about how you feel may leave you feeling like there is a lot more to explore.

To be clear, I am not suggesting that you should drop your ongoing therapy if you are in it and I am not recommending that you not try it if you have been contemplating it, but if this resonates, then like me, you have probably begun to master the art of talking about your difficult experiences without ever actually having to be in your body and feel them.

You will also recognise that this doesn't just show up in the therapeutic room and may even be more prominent in the relationships that mean the most to you. This is where it can truly create more painful cycles, leaving you feeling misunderstood as you become incapable of expressing your true feelings to the people you care most about. It's as if you go into hiding emotionally, that same childhood pattern of pushing your emotions down into your body and showing up in relationships as you think you need to. It can leave the people that you love in your life today feeling as though you are pushing them away or locking them out.

Awareness of all of this is not enough to curb it, and so it seeps into every aspect of your life. Emotional avoidance becomes the norm, and it is incredible what lengths you will go to in order to avoid feeling anything. Many people mistake this for resilience, or showing up without your emotions 'getting the better of you'. But there is a lot of denial in this. When you fail to process and express your emotions, they don't go away. In fact, you are storing them up in your body and having to work extra hard to face your day-to-day life, often preventing your nervous system from ever entering your relaxed state.

I want you to flip this narrative, and make your starting point one that hypothesises that you are feeling the way you are for perfectly legitimate and appropriate reasons. Then, with non-judgemental reflection and curiosity, know that you can start to hold and soothe yourself through the ways that you feel. You have way more power over it than you realise, and it can be enlightening. No longer will you ignore your body, but you will begin to listen to it and to trust what it is telling you. This is why you will develop your body first approach. You are going to retrain yourself to actively seek to be in your body and actively listen to what it is trying to tell you.

I want to encourage you to develop a deeper daily practice that supports this. There are so many practices to explore with this, and any somatic practice is worth exploring. In simple terms the 'soma' is the body, and so by somatic practice I mean anything that promotes your inward reflection of that. Obvious examples are meditation, yoga and even dance. If it brings your focus to your body and allows for the movement of your emotions, then it can be of benefit in this way. This is something that we know at a subconscious level but which we often ignore. Even when we don't ignore it, we don't seem to discuss the emotional benefits of dance or exercise in the way we should.

Meditation is often the practice that people highlight as being powerful for internal reflection. I have often struggled with meditation, though. Closing my eyes and being silent tends to send me straight to my stressed state. This makes sense in the context of my experience. When I was young and my brain was developing at its fastest rate, silence was often the quiet before the storm with my alcoholic dad. So, I believe my mind and body began to react to the world in this context. Is meditation something that you have tried before and, if so, how did you find the experience?

If my personal experience of meditation resonates with you in any way, then conscious connected breathing could be the perfect practice for you. Even if you don't identify with my meditation experiences, it is still a method that can bring you into your body and help support you in your body first approach. For me and so many others, it is the only way of being still in your body and allowing emotions to release.

Conscious connected breathing: how it works

Conscious connected breathing is a practice that is accessible to everyone and which can truly bring profound experiences in just one session. Learning about it has been revolutionary for me and for many others. When you breathe in a certain pattern for a prolonged period of time and stay connected, it takes you beyond your rational brain and into your body, and brings about life-changing experiences and emotional release. In simple terms it skips the part of you that works to keep you in your head, and sends you directly into your body. In many instances, you can release big, trapped emotions without even having to make too much rational sense of them.

CONSCIOUS CONNECTED BREATHWORK CAN HELP YOU BACK TO A PLACE WHERE BEING IN YOUR BODY FULLY FEELS SAFE AND MANAGEABLE.

This means that you have a much stronger chance of showing up more authentically. You can approach interactions in your relaxed state and feel more empowered to share your truth without fear of becoming overwhelmed. People regularly tell me that just one session can feel like 30 years of therapy!

EXERCISE: PRACTISING CONSCIOUS CONNECTED BREATHING

There are many different practices of conscious connected breathing, all taking on slightly different variations. My favourite is to breathe in through the mouth with a two-part inhale and then breathe out through the mouth too. Take in a nice big breath through your mouth, expanding your belly, and just as you feel your inhale is finished, pull another breath into your chest: this is the two-part inhale. Then simply let all of the air taken in fall out. You then go straight into the next inhale, repeating the process without resting in between. Repeat this for a period of around 20 minutes.

I am passionate about helping everyone start a journey with breathwork and I believe conscious connected breathing is the missing piece for a lot of people on their journey. Anyone can start practising it today and I want to help you realise how. Whether you are an expert in breathwork or have never tried it before, it can be an amazing way of coming into your body and helping you to start really letting go of stored-up feelings that you may otherwise not have been able to release. Building a relationship with the breath will be like opening the passage between your head and your heart and allowing you to drop back into your body in a way you haven't experienced before. It will help you to feel much more in charge of your nervous system. What follows a session is the ability to sit with your thoughts and feelings for a prolonged period of time.

You have already begun to practise some breathing patterns at the end of the first three chapters. Throughout the rest of this book, a full conscious connected breathing will become the way we close each chapter to help integrate with your body all of the work that you will do.

Before you do this, reflect again on each state of the nervous system and the thoughts you noted down for each one.

JOURNAL PROMPTS

By now you will hopefully have some detailed notes on what each state is like for you. This can become your nervous system map. Consider this as you complete the prompts below.

- How do you feel about committing to spending more time in your relaxed state?
- When working through each following chapter, as well as in your day-to-day life, take regular pauses to recognise what

state you are in and begin to note down what helps you in that state as well as what can have a negative impact. There aren't any one-size-fits-all approaches to moving through your nervous system map, but I do believe that, within you, you will know exactly what you need when you work towards better awareness of each state.

Breathwork

Now to put this into practice! You are going to practise a full conscious connected breathwork session, as you will do to close every forthcoming chapter. To do this, you will need to be somewhere comfortable and undisturbed. You will need to be lying down for this unless health reasons make this impossible. Use the QR code below to find the breathwork session.

5.
IT STARTS NOW

Most people who have endured a dysfunctional childhood wouldn't even know where to begin if they were asked, 'Who are you really?' Maybe this is something that you can relate to? It can be daunting when you have spent your life pandering to someone else's needs. The moment you began to develop a sense of self, the traits of your toxic parent meant that rather than becoming the person you were meant to be, you got lost in the person they needed you to be. You became an expert at being what everyone else needed. If I asked you what you needed to be for other people, such as for your partner or your friends, you would probably find it much easier to reel off some answers. This chapter will dive further into why this is.

Having previously gained some clarity around growing up with and managing a toxic parent in Chapters 1 and 2, beginning to build community though connection in Chapter 3, and then starting to feel more in control of your nervous system in Chapter 4, the knee-jerk reaction is to jump straight back and attempt to work with everything that happened when you were younger. This is also what so many healing modalities will suggest. As a result, it is easy to now get stuck in a loop of going over and over your childhood, believing that if you explore and understand it enough you will then free yourself from it. This can leave you trapped in a powerless loop. It is too late to go back and live a perfect childhood, but what you can do is actively work on the impact it has had on you. In this chapter you will gain some clarity around who you truly are and how there is an inner child within you today, whose champion you can work towards becoming.

One of the best ways to do this is to allow yourself to dream up what life would be like if nothing else mattered. Where would you be now if you hadn't spent a lifetime becoming what your parent needed? Who would you be if you could be the lead architect of your own perfect life? It is very likely that these questions alone leave you drawing a blank. Don't worry, you will dive deeper into this now.

Start by reflecting on the questions over the page, and see if you can start picturing what life would be like if you were to dream up the perfect one. If you can, don't just answer the questions but use them as a catalyst to dream up the life you might have had today if nothing else mattered. Don't overthink this, and don't let your mind stop you from writing what you truly want to. You don't have to show anyone what you write, so really run with this, and answer these questions solely with your own wants and desires in mind.

JOURNAL PROMPTS

- As a child, what was your biggest dream?
- If your life had followed the perfect path, where would you be now?
- What would you be doing?
- How would you feel?
- Who would be there?
- Who wouldn't be there?

Clear answers to these questions will help to create what we can call your perfect scene. However, as simple as the questions may seem on paper, they can unearth a lot for you. Notice the thought patterns you had. Did you find it difficult to simply answer what would be right for you? It is common for adult children of toxic parents to get in their own way here. Every thought of what they might want is met with another thought that renders it silly, or finds a reason why they shouldn't have that on their mind – and that's if you managed to access those thoughts at all. Many people find it difficult to even reach these thoughts, as they have buried their own needs so deeply. Don't worry if this is you. The breathwork at the end of this chapter will help you to unearth more of what you haven't been able to access within the reflections here.

Once upon a time, you had dreams. You may not even remember them, but you did. And I am not talking about an incessant yearning for something that you might never have, I am talking about what life could be like for you if you got to be the truest version of yourself. Maybe you dreamed of becoming a singer or an actor, but were told you couldn't sing or act. Maybe you wanted to be a parent yourself and dreamed of owning a big home with land and animals, but you were laughed at or ridiculed for the thought. Eventually you stopped dreaming, and you began to fall in line with the beat of your childhood. A toxic parent will have purposely sucked the hope out of you and the dysfunctional environment will have meant you lost touch with those dreams.

Your natural human desire to dream as a child will have been controlled both explicitly and implicitly by a toxic parent, and this meant that dreaming in any way was simply not accepted. Examples of how they will have explicitly done this would be directly ridiculing any dream you may have vocalised, or simply telling you in no uncertain terms that your dreams were impossible or completely unachievable. The more implicit ways will have been by forcing their own desires and life wants onto you, perhaps guilt-tripping you into thinking more in a way that suited them.

This is why it is important to see that your life was actually a gift to the world, and the role of your parent should have been to love and nurture you into growing into your innate value and discovering exactly who you are meant to be. Of course, every parent will fall short of this from time to time, but when you looked at the traits of a toxic parent in Chapter 1 and realised the extent of their toxicity, it will have been made clear that you were never parented into recognising your own value or following your dreams. But your dreams and aspirations are your greatest clues to exactly who you are meant to be.

Answering the questions that helped create your perfect scene will have offered clues to the person you were before the impact of a toxic parent took hold. The place you dreamed up, what you were doing, the people you were with – and the people you weren't with – they don't make you stupid or weird, and they don't have to be completely unobtainable in the way you were made to feel. However, it is likely that you have given up on your true self, and perhaps without even acknowledging that is the case.

That's what I did in my early teens. I stopped thinking about a life that I wanted and instead thought about a life that was manageable, or even survivable. My dreams were of being an actor, and I also really loved working to help people. I remember being in plays and receiving high praise for my acting abilities in the first few years of high school, but never fully being able to believe that praise. Never feeling like it was something worth following, or that would ever be reachable for me. As I moved towards my mid-teens that passion was squeezed out of me. I would have felt ridiculous even suggesting that I wanted to be an actor when I was older. Instead, I played it safe and not only let go of my dreams but began to bury them. Instead of my childhood being one where I explored who I was and who I wanted to be, it was more about working to become what I believed it was acceptable to be. I completely lost the ability at that time to reflect inwards on my wants and desires, let alone follow them.

This is common for people who grow up in dysfunction. It creates a constant internal feeling of being lost and unfulfilled that you will perhaps relate to. Looking back on the reflection you did in the previous chapter in which you pictured a young child, it will become clear how difficult it would have been to be yourself when it didn't align with what your toxic parent wanted. In particular, the dysfunction created by your toxic parent needing to be the centre of the universe at all times, as explored in Chapter 1, will have left no room for your exploration of yourself and your hopes and dreams. As a result, you will have been left with no choice but to bend and mould yourself into what worked within the dysfunctional system.

HOW YOU ABANDONED YOURSELF

Having to fit into that dysfunctional environment will have meant abandoning yourself and becoming what you needed to in order to survive within the dysfunctional family system. There are a number of ways you will have done that. Here are some of the most common ways that the children of toxic parents begin to abandon their true paths in this way. At least one of these will resonate with you strongly, and it is likely that they may all resonate in some way. As you go through these traits, reflect on how you show up to the world today.

People-pleasing

Can you think of the last time you did something for someone that you really didn't want to do just to please them?

How often do you apologise and take blame when it isn't your fault?

Do you find it almost impossible to say no to people?

People-pleasing is driven by the belief that the only way you can be lovable is by pleasing everyone around you. You may have even built a whole persona around how useful you can be to everyone else. On the face of it, this might seem like a noble way to live, but it is rooted in self-abandonment. You become completely incapable of checking in with yourself and your needs, and an expert at meeting everyone else's. This will have helped in the environment that you grew up in, as pleasing your toxic parent was the fastest route to survival, but it is problematic in your adult life as it consistently leaves your needs unmet. In your relationships today you likely feel lonely and misunderstood, as communicating your true self is forfeited in attempts to please people.

This means that you are very likeable. You may have lots of people around you who think very highly of you. Maybe you are the person everybody comes to with their problems. You always know what to say and what to do and how to be, and everybody says that you're so caring. However, being likeable is not the same as being liked. You create bonds with people based on what you think they need you to be. You work out what they're looking for and you make sure that you become that. They get a nice friendship with you but it's completely at the expense of yourself – you don't get connection from that in the way that you should. You may have lots of people in your life as a result of being likeable, but ultimately it leaves you feeling lonely. Yet it still feels like there's too much risk for you to be liked for who you actually are, because that will mean that some people won't like you, and your fear of abandonment is too strong.

How often are you abandoning yourself in an attempt to make everyone else feel OK?

What is the cost to you and others of your people-pleasing tendencies?

Of all of the traits listed here, people-pleasing is the most common in children raised by a toxic parent. As you will discover is the case with most of the other traits that follow, people-pleasing is a trait that you may have to reflect on a little to realise how much it is showing up in your life. Many people allow these traits to become ingrained within their personality and so it can be harder to see them for what they are.

Fixing

Do you feel like you have a skill for seeing the good in even the worst people? When was the last time you thought about how often this gets you hurt? You spend your life trying to fix and save everyone. You actively seek out people to do this with even if they don't need or want saving. You're drowning while holding people afloat. Your relationships are tainted by your incessant need to fix everything so as to avoid any pain arising. It is suffocating for you – and for the people you are trying to fix. As a child, you may have felt like you couldn't fix the way your parent was. This likely led to obsessively trying to fix yourself, before fixing people in relationships became more prevalent in adulthood. Today you may have found yourself entering relationships like a 'project' in an attempt to save the person you enter the relationship with, often leaving you vulnerable to more emotional hurt. Or it could show up more subtly. You find yourself constantly checking that people are OK and then taking responsibility for trying to make them 'better'.

As well as an attempt to fix yourself, I also believe it comes back to emotional avoidance. If you can fix the situation quickly, you'll never have to be in the difficult resulting emotion. That's why sometimes it can feel frantic, particularly with the people you care about the most. You are desperate to fix the situation as quickly as you can, to ensure that you avoid the emotion.

How often are you trying to fix other people?

How do you feel when your attempts to fix fail, or are not well received?

This is often a big trait for children of toxic parents. I certainly know myself to be a fixer, especially with the people I love, and, in my case, I know that it is driven by a fear of difficult emotions. It is worth spending some time here reflecting on your own desire to fix, and what really drives it. Go beyond the usual 'I just want everyone to be OK' line that is commonly used, and really challenge yourself to go a bit further in your reflection.

Perfectionism

When was the last time that you allowed yourself to just be enough? Do you have a need to ace everything, and, if you feel like you can't, do you prefer not to start? Perfectionism is simply the need for everything to be completely perfect. All your attention and focus goes into this. It ultimately leaves you feeling like a failure at everything, as you set a bar that you never reach. A childhood that was steeped in dysfunction left you feeling devoid of any control. Attempting to perfect everything was an opportunity to claw back some of that control. As an adult it can become almost paralysing, preventing you from pursuing paths that you deserve to follow, and leaving you feeling like nothing that you do is ever good enough.

What areas of your life does perfectionism show up in?

How does it feel when you believe you haven't been perfect?

It's worth exploring beyond some of the narratives that you may already have around your perfectionism. It is common to tell ourselves stories that help hide traits like this. You might suggest that you 'just like things to be done properly', but if you were to dig a bit deeper and ask yourself why that is you may discover more than you expect.

Shrinking

Have you ever hidden in a situation? Has your very existence ever felt like it is getting in the way and, as a result, you have shrunk to be as small as you can? I am talking not just about your physical being here but about your personality and who you are. You have become an expert at playing small and blending in, and over time, you have likely withdrawn as much as possible. You isolate a lot and, when you do have to interact with others, you try not to take up too much space. Instead you blend into the background as much as possible. This can be common if your childhood home had a lot of chaos and you tried to stay out of the 'firing line'. In adulthood you find yourself apologising all the time for things that really don't warrant an apology. It also means that you miss out on so much of what you deserve from life, surviving instead of thriving.

Shrinking is normalised within our society, and you will be celebrated as being easygoing. Standing in your power, being exactly who you're supposed to be and having clear boundaries is often seen as arrogant or abrasive, and so shrinking can seem like an easier option.

Do you show up as your full self in the company of others?

Are you shrinking in any of your relationships today?

How does shrinking resonate with you? It could be that this lands wholeheartedly and you recognise this as you in a nutshell! For others, there may be a sense that it doesn't resonate at all. If you are the latter, I would really focus on the questions around shrinking in your relationships. You may still find that this one doesn't resonate with you, or you may begin to see that in certain relationships parts of who you are do go into hiding. It is really common for adult children of toxic parents to be quite big and extroverted in their day-to-day life but to slowly shrink over time within their meaningful relationships, particularly their romantic ones. This can be very lonely and isolating.

Self-sabotage

How often during times that should rationally feel great do you want to mess it all up? Those are the more explicit ways of self-sabotage. You hit the self-destruct button and send your life crashing down when it was seemingly all going so well. It can be more subtle than that, too. Actively avoiding moments in life that you know could help improve your situation, or partaking in things that will obviously slowly deteriorate it. As a child, your toxic parent may have actively sought to remove things from your life that would have created joy for you. Even if this wasn't the case for you, the unpredictability of the dysfunction meant that you dared not enjoy positive moments too much, because they were often the calm before the storm. Thinking about your nervous system map from the previous chapter, self-sabotage can often relate to the discomfort of the survival state. You self-sabotage because you don't know how to self-soothe.

It may be that when everything is calm and just as it is supposed to be, you become anxious. You're constantly wondering when this good feeling is going to end. That's where the anxiety comes from. When will this be snatched away from you? When will this moment of joy or freedom come crashing down? The worry of that happening becomes so overwhelming that you hit that self-destruct button yourself and seek comfort from things falling down around you and you having to rebuild them.

Are there any current or recent times when you feel you may have self-sabotaged?

Can you think of any time when you didn't put your all into something positive, and lost out as a result?

Before I found sobriety, I was very actively self-sabotaging, I was almost openly doing it. Sobriety hasn't completely eradicated that behaviour either. I am still very capable of self-sabotage, but today it is often more subtle for me and perhaps not as extreme. How is it showing up for you in your life today or recently?

Addiction/escapism

How often do you reach for something in an attempt to take you away from this moment? When you're in your stressed or survival state do you look for a substance or behaviour in an attempt to soothe?

I believe that addiction is simply obsessive escapism. When being in the moment is simply too painful, you will find a way to escape it. Remembering what you explored with the nervous system in Chapter 3, if you find yourself trapped in the stressed or survival state, then obsessively seeking escapism makes sense. If you imagine a scale of desire to escape, I will say that we all sit somewhere on that scale, and anything near the higher end of that could be considered addiction.

There are the more obvious addictions to alcohol and drugs, and there are many more subtle ones too. In many ways, all of the traits we are discussing here are addictions in their own right, but it may be that you spend your life leaning on something to escape reality and it takes over a lot of your life. It doesn't have to be a substance like alcohol or even food – it could be behaviours, too. For example, being addicted to work or difficult relationships is extremely common and can be very debilitating. Many people actively, albeit subconsciously, pick addictive behaviours that people are less likely to call out. I am the master of this! Helping people, specifically by leading spaces, is the most common place I seek escape.

Escapism likely started for you younger than you can remember in attempts to protect yourself from the toxicity, but it may have developed into stronger, more addictive behaviours in adulthood. Most people are doing something in an attempt to escape their reality and, in some ways, I would argue we all need a little bit of that, but it is important to reflect on your more prevalent addictive behaviours and become curious about their existence.

What behaviours in your life bring you temporary relief but in the long run cause you harm or set you back in your life, but you continue to do anyway?

What behaviours are you relying on too heavily, which if removed would leave you feeling completely overwhelmed?

This will be easier to spot in some behaviours than others, and I encourage you to get curious enough to explore more than one behaviour. In my case, it is relatively easy for me to look back at my relationship with alcohol and see that it only brought temporary relief, it had a negative impact in the long run, and that I was relying on it too heavily. That certainly doesn't mean it was easy to stop, but the issue is more recognisable. However, when it comes to me helping people, it can be much easier to hide those three key things. If I am willing to dive a bit deeper with myself, I can see that helping people does bring me relief from the more difficult emotions. It may not always directly have a negative impact in the long run, but I can be guilty of helping people or supporting my family in times of need, and I most certainly dive into helping others as a coping mechanism that I lean on all too much.

With some reflection, can you see that you may relate to some of the traits listed above? The common thread is a disconnection from your true self. Rather than a fixed belief that this is just the way that you are, can you begin to see that these traits make sense within the context of life with your toxic parent? It is extremely common for people to believe that they have no control over these personal traits, as if there is nothing that can be done about them. The opposite is actually the case. Full acceptance that these traits were born in reaction to your dysfunctional childhood may be too difficult to digest, but it also shows that, as a reaction to your experiences, they absolutely can be overridden.

This is why you start in the now. It isn't that you need to rid yourself entirely of these traits, but more that you can become aware of when they show up. Remember that you have power over them and that you can navigate most situations without the need to abandon yourself entirely.

The common fear here is of who you are without these traits, but behind them all is your inner child. This is the part of you that you have spent your lifetime protecting. It is an internal part that you may have buried so deep you don't even know exists, but I can assure you it does. These traits actively keep it hidden and protect it at all costs. You may do this consciously or it may be subconscious, but they are all an attempt to protect that inner child. Think back to when you explored loneliness in Chapter 3. Your inner child is that part of you around which you have built a fortress.

In a moment you are going to gently try to picture the earliest version of you that you can remember. This may feel like a stretch for you, and that is OK. If you cannot visualise clearly, you may try to conjure up a memory from a photograph. If it is still a struggle, then you can visualise your own child or simply just a young child. If you still struggle to get a picture in your mind, then just get a sense of existence for this little version of you. We will now refer to this as the 'little you'. That little you was full of hope of life. They still believed in the power of the moment and of presence. They did not self-organise or check whether how they presented was going to be acceptable; they were completely authentic. More on authenticity after this next exercise.

EXERCISE: INNER CHILD VISUALISATION

Sit or lie comfortably with a straight back. Close your eyes and take some breaths in through your nose, elongating the exhale. Take four seconds to breathe in through your nose and seven seconds to breathe out through your mouth. While repeating this pattern, gently picture the little you. Don't rush this part, just spend some time trying to visualise or feel this part of you that you have worked so hard to protect. Try to see their face, their eyes, their hair and their body in your mind. There is no desired outcome here, just notice. I encourage you to stick with this exercise for a minimum of five minutes. You may find that your mind does all that it can to prevent you from succeeding in your visualisation here.

When you feel you have given this your best shot, get a pen and some paper, look at the journal prompts below, and note down what comes up for you. You may need to repeat the reflecting process for each question, noting whatever comes into your head each time. Again, I encourage you to make time for this and continue with the breathing pattern, even when you are writing down your reflections.

JOURNAL PROMPTS

- What did you feel when you tried to picture the little you?
- Where in your body was activated the most?
- What did you sense little you was feeling?
- What did they want?

You may have noticed a difficulty visualising the little you, or that when you saw them in your mind, they were uncomfortable in your presence. I have worked with so many people who have dived headfirst into working with their inner child and found that the results left them feeling frustrated at best. Working towards becoming someone that your inner child can feel safe in the presence of is the biggest part of this work, and is often the part that most miss out. That work is focused on you and who you are today. It is like doing the training before delving in and trying to reparent yourself.

That little you is still there and is part of who you are. Through this work, you'll come to understand how much you need and deserve a relationship with them. You will see that this work is worth doing for yourself and for your inner child. Nobody ever held that little you and helped them navigate through the struggle, but you will get to be that person. As a result, you will re-establish a connection with them that is so deep you become the authentic person you were always meant to be.

AUTHENTICITY

A lot is said within the wellbeing space when it comes to the importance of authenticity. In most cases people simply equate it to just 'being yourself'. But what does that mean when you have no idea who you truly are? Let me offer you a much clearer idea of what authenticity is. Authenticity is when you are able to know exactly what you are feeling, know exactly what you need as a result of what you are feeling, and then know how to communicate that need to the people who matter. In this way, babies are completely authentic. They are present in the moment and never question whether they should cry in order to get what they want. As they grow into their life, however, and they develop their sense of self, they will begin to adapt to what gets them the most acceptance from the person whose role it is to meet their needs: their parent. This is where so many people's insecurities come from. Even those raised in the most functional of environments will begin to adapt accordingly in order to receive acceptance from their parents or carers. If, as a child, one notices their mum's face tighten whenever they display their sadness, then that child will begin to look for ways to adapt and not show their sadness.

In Chapter 4 we explored how, as the child of a toxic parent, you had to disconnect from your body and stay in your head, rationalising things. We have now also explored some of the traits you may have taken on too, and in the coming chapters you will learn even more about how you journeyed away from your authentic self.

Can you reflect on your childhood experiences? Are there any events or moments that may have led you away from your authenticity in the way I have just described?

It may be that your childhood memories are so faint that you draw a blank here. Try then to hypothesise. Considering the picture that you have developed of your parent from the traits you explored in Chapter 1, and coupling that with the visualisation of your inner child that you have done within this chapter, can you hypothesise what that little you might have experienced at the hands of a parent with the toxic traits that you recognise in your parent now?

I find it difficult to adequately recall much of my childhood and so I have to hypothesise, particularly when thinking about my formative years. I know my home was often chaotic and full of big emotions. Whether it was my dad's drunken rage or my mum's desperate sadness as a result of my dad's behaviour, there was no space for me to externalise any of my feelings. I remember crying a lot on my own in my room and not really understanding why. I also remember really wanting to show my mum that I was OK. I can draw connections here to the origins of my people-pleasing, and it helps me to see it more compassionately.

I have more vivid memories of my teenage years – at least vivid memories of the ways that I felt; actually recalling events and remembering them in order to recite them gets a little trickier. My teenage years are when I truly began to self-organise. I was extremely conscious of how I showed up and would rapidly edit how I spoke, looked and acted in an attempt to be acceptable. This was mainly directed towards my peers, though. As is common for those with a degree of trauma in childhood, I struggled with authority figures, and every adult felt like one of those to me. I was so desperate to be accepted by the people around me and so desperately conscious of how different I felt to all of them. I remember feeling very different from everybody else. Not in a rational sense, though. It wasn't that I looked at other people's lives and thought that mine was very different. I just felt like a very different person. I always felt nobody understood me. I can see today a lot of that is to do with my sensitivity, but much of it was also driven by shame over the years in high school. I changed friendship groups regularly. I would move around in a desperate attempt to be accepted, and I would change my style and personality completely if it felt needed. From the way I looked to the way I dressed, anything to be accepted by another group of people.

I use the word 'healing' a lot, but a lot of this work is about recovery. Recovering that little you in all their incredible uniqueness and innocence and reconnecting them with the person that you have become today.

Within this chapter, you will have begun to establish that many of the ways you show up in your life today make sense when explored in the full context of your life as the child of a toxic parent. You have coupled that with the realisation of your inner child, and how you have spent much of your life trying to protect them. In the coming chapters you will dive further into the work on who you are today, which will help recover the connection to that little you, and as a result you will become the most authentic version of you.

JOURNAL PROMPTS

- Which ways to abandon yourself have you been using the most?
- What commitment can you make to help stay in your authenticity?
- How does it feel to begin to see your inner child more clearly?

Breathwork

Before moving on, create some time and space to complete the conscious connected breathwork session and visualisation for this chapter. Having completed your first full session at the end of the previous chapter, you can now use the words of affirmation that you will hear in the recording throughout the breathwork routine to support the work within the chapters. The visualisations will also become a huge part of bringing everything together. In this session you will be taken to your perfect scene where you will again picture that little you. Use the QR code below to complete this breathwork.

6. SELF-COMPASSION

How often does the voice in your head shame you for even the simplest of mistakes?

How often do you blame yourself for all of your struggles?

Growing up with a toxic parent displaying all of the traits we explored in Chapter 1 leaves most people with an almost debilitating self-talk. Think about the way that you talk to yourself, particularly when you feel you have messed up. Would you ever speak to others in that way? Despite everything that you have been through, you are still much harder on yourself than on anyone else. Imagine a close friend sharing a story that was similar to yours. Would you say the same things to them? Would you tell them that they should have been stronger or that they brought a lot of the experiences on themself? I can almost certainly predict that you wouldn't. So, why is it so difficult to not aim this type of shaming self-talk at yourself? Why do you think you find it so much easier to regard other people's experiences with more compassion, and help them see that they have been doing their best or that they wouldn't have got to where they are now if they didn't have any strength?

Self-compassion is the ability to find some empathy and understanding towards yourself, particularly in tough times. Many people find this difficult and don't realise that much of the reason for this is because hidden in their subconscious is the belief that they are defined only by their mistakes. In this chapter, we are going to look deeper at why you have shown up in the way that you have throughout your adulthood, what that has meant, and how you can start to view that through the lens of self-compassion. You will discover the ability to empathise with yourself in the way you often empathise with others. It is time to turn some of that compassion inwards. You will do this by taking a clear look at many of the mistakes that you have made throughout your life and, despite how difficult that might seem, finding the courage to see them in their entirety.

EXERCISE: SELF-COMPASSION MIRROR REFLECTION

Start by reflecting on where you are when it comes to self-compassion. Take a moment to think about how it feels to empathise with who you are right now.

Next, find a comfortable sitting position in front of a mirror so you can see your face. Use the four-second inhale, seven-second exhale we discussed in the previous chapter and let your mind turn towards empathy and compassion for who you are right now. While using the breathing pattern, look directly into your own eyes in the mirror and repeat, either out loud or in your mind, 'I forgive you.'

Reflective work that uses a mirror while focusing on your breathing can give you profound insight into how you see yourself. You may find it extremely difficult to hold your own gaze and your body may become quite activated, in that you may begin to feel different sensations within your body. As suggested in Chapter 4, notice these as much as you can and reflect on what message your body is trying to deliver. Don't judge any of what comes up or jump straight to fixing it - just note with honesty what is there. We can return to this at the end of the chapter, when you will have more clarity.

JOURNAL PROMPTS

- Jot down some notes on what you noticed in the last exercise. Take into account how you felt when speaking into the mirror and saying, 'I forgive you.' How often do you forgive yourself? How did it feel to look yourself in the eye and say those words? Was it awkward? Did you resist your own gaze? What do you think this tells you about how compassionately you see yourself? If you were forgiving of yourself, this reflective exercise will have been a warm and inviting experience. You will have felt a deep acceptance of what you were saying to yourself, and felt it easy to hold your own gaze.
- If others knew everything about you, how do you think they would view you? Just be honest here. You could think of your three closest friends, and simply list some things they might say if they had to describe you. There is no desired outcome

here, just see what it brings up for you and how you feel as a result.

- If you had to list some words that best described you, what would they be? As words come to you, write them down without too much thought. You may find that some words feel contradictory and that part of you says one thing while another part thinks the opposite. This is normal, and you will explore why this is so in Chapter 7.

SHAME

As we discussed in the previous chapter, it is important to work with the person that you are right now. You may have so much shame rushing around your head as a reaction to your experiences in life that jumping back to your childhood wouldn't work, and that little you wouldn't feel safe in your company if you are still lost in your shame.

Shame is the deep-rooted idea that something is wrong with you. Embarrassment is part of this, but shame is more than that. Everybody experiences shame from time to time. It is when you hide certain parts of yourself, terrified of what people might think. It could be a behaviour, a feeling or just a glancing thought, but when you experience it you might hope for it to stay secret forever, with an underlying belief that if someone knew you had that experience, they would hate you too. That's shame. It is common for children who have grown up in dysfunction to become shame-based. This is when one feels so much shame, they carry the belief that they must hide every part of themself. It becomes self-defeating, as the way to combat shame is to have the parts of yourself that feel shame be seen clearly by yourself and by others.

How much shame do you think you are carrying?

Did the self-compassion mirror reflection and the journal prompts teach you anything about your own shame?

You have the courage needed to do this because that is why you are here. You may not feel or see that, but you do: purchasing this book and beginning this work is not the act of someone lacking in courage. It also proves that somewhere within you there is a part of you that knows you deserve more, because why else would you be doing this? I ask that you harness that for this part of the journey. The self-compassion mirror reflection will have highlighted some of the shame you are carrying, and it is normal as you take on the upcoming work which will now get even deeper, for that shame to heighten the fear within you. Be gentle with yourself, but know that your fear of the work is very appropriate and very human.

FORGIVENESS

To truly forgive someone is to release yourself from blame, resentment and anger so that you can be free – however they wronged you. The route to self-compassion is through forgiveness, but forgiveness is an overused term. It is thrown around in the healing space as if it is something that can be achieved by the click of your fingers. It is an ultimate ideal, and it is suggested that if you can reach forgiveness in any situation then you are more healed than those who cannot. Let's dispel that myth immediately. There are people in my life who have hurt me who I have not forgiven and who hold no power over me whatsoever. In other cases, forgiveness has shown up for me, but it is only as the result of the work that I have done on myself. I don't believe it is possible to just forgive; it comes as a by-product of other self-work. I also don't believe it is essential to forgive anyone in your life. Even your parent. Forgiveness of others is not the only route to freedom from their hurt. That may come as a relief to you, or it may feel uncomfortable, but it is the reality.

This is something else you will have likely had pushed on you if you dare to speak about the toxicity of your parent: that you should just simply forgive them, irrespective of the level abuse and regardless of whether the abuse is still happening. This isn't a fair ask. Again, somewhere along the journey of healing you may land at forgiveness, and that is great, but it is not a 'must'.

Forcing forgiveness can be detrimental for you having grown up with a toxic parent. It can serve to downplay the level of pain that you have experienced at the hands of someone who may even, in many cases, still be trying to abuse you. It is important to honour your feelings for what they are and not to feel pressured to be working towards new ones. Forcing yourself to move towards forgiveness can cloud your judgement and leave you more vulnerable to the abusive manipulation.

It is simply more of the same spiritual bypassing that is a common trait of a toxic parent. It is an attempt to avoid the discomfort that comes with difficult emotions. I have been there. Sweeping my true feelings under the carpet and spouting ideas of forgiveness and letting go. It doesn't work like that. I understand why it happens – to force yourself to believe you have reached forgiveness is a more comfortable path than the one full of discomfort that comes with the truth of your experience. This is avoidance, though, and becomes another barrier to you being able to be in your body in the way you need, as explored in Chapter 4.

Self-forgiveness, however, is something I want to encourage you to think about. This is the only form of forgiveness that it is essential you work towards. It won't come from me telling you it is needed, nor will it arrive even if *you* fully believe in its need, but self-forgiveness is something I encourage you to aim for. And you will take a huge leap towards it as a by-product of the work in this chapter. However, it will feel like a daunting task.

If you were to think of the biggest mistake you have made in your life, how would forgiving yourself for that feel? Maybe you hurt some of the people you care about the most, or you failed in a relationship that you really cared about? Maybe you didn't follow the career you desired, or stayed in a relationship that you shouldn't have? Even if you have the desire to forgive yourself for these things, the route to finding true forgiveness is often hard to see. This was certainly true for me at this stage of my journey. I had no idea where to begin. My self-hatred ran so deep that I wasn't even sure I wanted to forgive myself at all.

My self-loathing came from knowing I had hurt the people I love the most – my children. I had always dreamed of having children and being a good father. I had dreamed of it most of my life. To have lots of children, and not be an alcoholic like my dad. When I held my daughter in my arms for the first time, I remember being overcome with love. I am not sure I had felt anything like that before, not for anyone. I couldn't quite comprehend the love I was experiencing. I vividly remember the very physical feeling of that love. It rushed over me, that warm, fuzzy feeling that takes over your whole body and goes beyond words. But that feeling was all too quickly replaced with self-hatred because, as I looked at my daughter who was only hours old and was staring back at me, my overwhelming thought was that she would need to get as far away from me as possible because she deserved a real shot at life, and I would only be able to offer the opposite. For a number of years, those fears became a reality. My relationship with alcohol and my behaviours around that caused my daughter and my other children pain before I got sober, and that I can never take back.

Perhaps my experiences are extreme, but the way I dealt with them are most certainly not. It is very common to get caught in the trap of pushing down the full truth of your experience, as it is too painful to bear, and doing so means that you can never fully move through it. As we learned in Chapter 4, when we cannot process and release those emotions, they don't go away and instead influence how we see ourselves and the world. It is like spending your life desperately running from a storm cloud, terrified of being caught in the rain, when in reality if you stopped, your experience would be more difficult for a short period of time until the cloud passed over you and you became free.

Seeing your mistakes and all the things that you have done that leave you feeling shameful is undoubtably a scary proposition, but it is essential to any healing journey. If you are to work through your experiences in the fullness that is needed, then you have to see all of your experiences for what they are. This doesn't happen for most people. Instead, emotionally avoidant narratives are created to help people continue to run from their storm cloud.

EMOTIONALLY AVOIDANT NARRATIVES

Emotionally avoidant narratives are the phrases, sentences and stories we use to avoid having to process or vocalise our difficult truths. They are usually statements that are positive in nature that help you to avoid the truth and, as a result, the discomfort that sometimes comes with that. We can all be guilty of emotionally avoidant narratives in difficult circumstances, as they can buy us short-term gain at the price of long-term pain. However, they are most often used when reflecting on our own mistakes. We might say things like, 'It really wasn't that bad,' when in reality we know that it was. Or we may dress things up slightly, saying, 'I acted a certain way in order to teach myself a lesson,' when, deep down, we actually feel shame around our actions.

As you go through life, you use these phrases and narratives more and more and they play a huge part in losing who you truly are. They become a barrier to self-awareness. By seeing the full truth of your experiences, you pierce through the emotionally avoidant narratives, and this is where you can truly begin to forgive yourself. This is where self-compassion becomes possible.

As I mentioned earlier in this chapter, forgiving yourself is vital. Not only that, but you also deserve it. You are not a bad person just because you may have made some mistakes.

Self-forgiveness will come when you walk through the storm and fully release yourself from your mistakes. So much of your parent's toxicity comes from their unwillingness to self-reflect in any way. You are going to do the opposite. That is not always easy, but it is important to recognise the need to be completely honest with yourself about your mistakes and the actions you have taken as an adult. Most people are gritting their teeth and hoping that their difficult feelings around some of those actions simply go away. They don't. They live inside you and impact how you see yourself and how you relate to the world and the people in it. To have any chance of being authentically you as described in the previous chapter, you must release yourself from the chains of your mistakes.

EXERCISE: A LETTER TO THE LITTLE YOU

You are going to write a letter to the little you that you visualised in Chapter 5, apologising for all the mistakes that you have made as an adult and that you feel have caused you harm. If you are still struggling to get a clear vision of the little you, that's OK, just know that you are writing to your younger self. You should specifically do this in letter format so that it feels personal. Imagine that the little you will be receiving and reading the letter. Really *feel* into it and, as emotions come up when writing, try to articulate them within the letter. When apologising for certain actions or events, allow yourself to write why you are sorry for it, and what it made you feel. It is important that you allow what you have felt around all of the instances you have buried to flow out in the letter.

Reflect on your mistakes only from around age 18, and work forwards from there. I don't want you to start much earlier than 18 because you were a child before that age. It is important not to take responsibility for too many things you did when you were a child and when you were deserving of more support. It may be that there are some significant things that happened in your mid- to late teens that you feel you want to get out, and that is OK. But for clarity, I don't want you apologising for anything that you did in reaction to the abuse that happened or the toxicity you faced when you were a child. That is why, here, I want you to focus on your adulthood as much as possible.

Be as thorough as you can. You might talk about failed relationships that you have had in adulthood. Maybe they ended too soon, or maybe they ended when they shouldn't have at all, and you believe the reasons for that were a lot to do with your actions within the relationship. You could talk about a career that ended or a job that you lost through mistakes that you made. You could talk about some of the people you love that you have hurt through some of your actions. Maybe you pushed them away, acted foolishly, or treated them with less love than they deserved. You could also explore apologising for some of the things you haven't done that you should have, like putting yourself and your needs first.

This might be a difficult or heavy exercise for you, but you are not here to beat yourself up. Writing the letter is about drawing a line in the sand. Your secrets keep you alone in the world and they also keep you separate from yourself. Your secrets are often secrets because you are so terrified and ashamed of them, you dare not let others see what you do when you examine them.

> So, as uncomfortable as it is to get it all out, doing so is a step towards freedom. No more hiding from yourself. Once you have written the letter, hold on to it - you will use it when taking inventory later in this chapter.
>
> When we use the letter-writing format in this way, the idea is to try and get into that flow state of pouring your heart out. Don't overthink it - it isn't an assignment or school homework. It really doesn't matter if there are missing words, or if it is grammatically off. What matters is that you get it out. So, put pen to paper and get flowing.

How did it feel to get that all out? Like me, you will have been carrying so much shame as a result of some things you have done in your adulthood. You have pushed the thoughts and feelings of what you have done down into your body, and that is where they have been trapped. It becomes part of your being, part of the way that you see yourself and even how you view the world. This was so true for me. Even after I had found sobriety, I had to stay hidden. I found it impossible to look myself and other people in the eye because I was terrified of what they might see. If you relate to that on some level, the purpose of the work within this chapter is designed to break through that shame.

Writing the letter in this way is the first step to getting out of your closet, but it may not yet feel better. In some ways, it may feel even worse to see it all written out. That is completely understandable. This exercise is about getting it all out. Shame cannot survive in the light, and while these things bounce around in your mind and body they prevent you from connecting with that little you in the way that will free you.

JOURNAL PROMPTS

This entire journey is about reaching a place where you can truly connect with your inner child, that little you. In the previous chapter, you spent time visualising them and now you have gone a step further and written them a letter. Now, take some time to reflect on the impact this has had by using the prompts below.

- If the little you were to describe you now, how do you think it would differ to how they would have described you before you wrote the letter?
- How does your visualisation of the little you now differ from before you wrote the letter?
- Closing your eyes and picturing them, are you able to make eye contact with the little you? What does it feel like?
- Thinking of the body first approach, where is most activated and how when you picture the little you? What can you learn from this?

It is difficult to love yourself when you are hiding who you are from such a core part of yourself. When you connect fully with your inner child, love for yourself flows naturally. You are working towards helping your inner child to feel completely safe within your company. Taking the truth from something that internally feels like a tangled mess to something that you have untangled and processed is going to help the little you feel safer in your company. You have more work to do, but you are making huge strides already.

TAKING PERSONAL INVENTORY

The letter you wrote to the little you was designed to connect you with emotions that you have buried and hidden as a result of some of your actions. As well as that, you are going to take inventory. Inventory can have a profound impact on how you perceive yourself and some of the mistakes you have made. Unlike the letter you wrote, this process is more of a fact-finding one. Though it is also about exploring some of the feelings behind the behaviours, it is less about leaning in to those feelings and more about discovering the reasons behind them. I first discovered inventory with the work that I did within Alcoholics Anonymous, and the impact for me was life-changing.

The three key elements to taking personal inventory are (1) taking responsibility for your actions as an adult, (2) finding some acceptance around the person you have become, and (3) exploring some changes that you can make to grow into the person you were always meant to be. Taking accountability for the person you are today is not always easy or comfortable work. As the child of a toxic parent, you didn't cause this – it is not your fault, but you do have a responsibility to work towards healing in the now. Acceptance will come through the understanding you will gain from reflecting on what was driving your actions, and the changes that you will need to make will be easier to spot as a result.

Everything will make so much more sense when you take inventory. It is not easy, and that is why most people avoid doing it. It is not something you hear of the average person doing. However, it is the surest way of committing yourself to breaking the cycle of dysfunction and being able to hold yourself accountable.

EXERCISE: TAKING PERSONAL INVENTORY

It is time to look again at the letter that you wrote to the little you earlier on in this chapter. Read through the letter, pulling out everything that you have apologised for and writing this down in a list. Then, you are going to create a table with three more columns alongside your list:

What was driving you?

What were you trying to do?

What should you have done?

It's important you use the table format, as this part of the work is about spotting patterns in your behaviours and your reactions to experiences. Rather than leaning in to your emotions too much, imagine you are zooming out and taking more of a clinical look at your mistakes. You will begin to see that, in the full context of your experience, they all make clearer sense.

On the next page is an example of how your table might look. It really doesn't matter how long your list is. You might have a huge list, or you might struggle to write much at all. Neither is better or worse. What is important is that you get it out. Take a look at the example table opposite, and then before reading on, create your own version.

MISTAKE	WHAT WAS DRIVING YOU?	WHAT WERE YOU TRYING TO DO?	WHAT SHOULD YOU HAVE DONE?
Over-isolating	Fear Self-loathing Abandonment	Cope Escape Survive	Been more open about my struggle and got support and connection from friends
Got into and stayed in relationships that hurt me	Fear Abandonment Shame Self-loathing Low self-esteem	Be wanted and loved Not be alone	Found support in the relationships that do value me Found ways to be happy alone
Not showing up as a parent	Fear Self-seeking	Survive Escape	Tried to be more present
Not following a career that I desired	Fear Shame No self-belief Self-loathing	Survive Escape Avoid failing	Found support Invested in myself Allowed myself to fail

JOURNAL PROMPTS

- Looking at your own table now, what patterns can you see?
- Can you summarise the main things that were driving you to the mistakes that you made?
- Can you summarise the main things that you were trying to do?
- Using the final column, are there learnings from the things that you should have done that you can use to help you evolve now?

Some of what you have discovered may have been things that you were already aware of, but maybe seeing it all laid out provides a moment of clarity? It is likely that you have spent a lot of your adulthood believing this is just the way you are. Taking inventory in this way will hopefully allow you to recognise that, like so many others in your situation, you have been reacting to the world the best way you can based on your experience. It is an incredible way to take responsibility for the here and now. Inventory in this way is known as 'cleaning your side of the street'.

Think about your experiences in childhood and the toxicity or dysfunction that you faced as a child. Doesn't it make sense that you showed up to adulthood in the way that you have? I'm not asking that you shift blame or responsibility here, I am simply encouraging you to look for some understanding and recognition of why you made the mistakes you did. This is the journey to self-compassion. In most contexts, I don't like the word 'blame'.

It suggests that there is one culprit in any misfortune. It's never that simple, but understanding and acknowledging the role of your childhood experiences at the hands of a toxic or dysfunctional parent, along with an acceptance of your own part which you've played as an adult, is what will evoke self-compassion that will run parallel to taking responsibility for who you are today.

The taking of inventory in this way is a fundamental part of any healing journey. It is not about self-shaming; it is about being able to see your experience in its entirety and begin to take back control over how you respond to the world, as a result of the things that happened to you. You are not a bad person. You may have done some bad things, but you are not a bad person. Acknowledgement of this will hand you back some power and help you towards more self-compassion.

You can bring this new-found knowledge into your day-to-day life, too. There will still be times going forward when you make mistakes and behave in ways you'd prefer not to. In those moments, you can take some inventory, gain an understanding of why they happened, and find some acceptance and self-compassion as a result. I would encourage you to begin to take some regular inventory too. You can do this daily or three to five times a week. During the evening can be a perfect time for this and can help you keep on top of things.

Now revisit the self-compassion mirror reflection. Using the four-second inhale and seven-second exhale that you are now familiar with, take some time to look yourself in the eye again, saying out loud or in your head, 'I forgive you.' How different does this now feel? Are you able to hold your own gaze more freely?

JOURNAL PROMPTS

Take another look at the journal prompts that followed the self-compassion mirror reflection.

- Has your view of self-forgiveness evolved since you completed this exercise?
- If others were completely honest and knew everything about you, how do you think they would view you?
- If you had to list some words that best described you, what would they be?

Compare your answers here to the answers you gave for the journal prompts that followed the mirror reflection on page 118. Has there been some evolution? Maybe seeing yourself in a new and different light has prompted you to believe that others see you differently. It could be that the way that you view yourself now matches more closely with how you feel others see you. Again, there is no right or wrong here, just curiosity around what you discover.

The true meaning of self-compassion is having the ability to find self-acceptance and understanding in our difficult times of failure or through hurt. It isn't always the absence of difficult feelings towards ourselves, but rather about an inner knowing that, with the right reflection, we can still feel loving towards ourselves in spite of any perceived difficult experience. This loving feeling replaces the barrage of self-criticising and leaves much less room for shame.

Having discovered that the only form of forgiveness that is truly needed is self-forgiveness, you have been able to explore a lot of the shame you have been holding as a result of growing up with a toxic parent. You have learned that the self-compassion mirror reflection is a great way to discover where you are in regards to your ability to see yourself through a loving lens. You can allow this to become a regular practice. It can be great for any morning routine, helping you to never stray too far from the self-compassion lens. Having really leant in to the feelings and emotions that surrounded your mistakes in life using the letter to your little you, you have been able to take a thorough inventory of your failings as an adult. By discovering clear patterns in your behaviour, this powerful practice helped you to see that, despite doing some bad things, you are not a bad person. This evokes the self-understanding and acceptance needed to become more loving in the way you see yourself. You are discovering true self-compassion.

JOURNAL PROMPTS

- What has been the biggest discovery of this chapter?
- What practices will you take from this chapter and make part of your routine?
- What is one clear change that you can now make to take more ownership over how you react to life?

Breathwork

Once you have answered these questions, it is time to breathe and come into your body to complete the cycle. Once again, you will complete a conscious connected breathing exercise with visualisation. This will focus on the self-compassion journey that you are now on. Give yourself some time and space to feel you have connected and explored the work fully in this chapter, and then use the QR code below to complete the breathwork.

7.
MEETING EVERY VERSION OF YOU

Do you ever feel like you don't know which version of yourself is the most authentic? This is one of the most common reasons people stay stuck at the beginning of their healing journey. There is an almost subconscious knowledge that, if they stop and reflect too much, they will not like what they see behind the roles they currently play in their day-to-day life. Sound familiar?

You're not alone and it is not just children of toxic parents who hide behind what can feel like masks; everyone does. Even if they don't realise it, they do. Everybody has slightly different versions of themselves that show up in different scenarios within their life. For some it may be quite subtle, but for many others it can be quite drastic. The amount of dysfunction that someone experiences in childhood can be an indicator of just how drastically different each version of themself can be.

In this chapter, we are going to look more closely at who you become in different situations, whether that's at work, with your friends or with your partner, and how you can learn to recognise and love all versions of yourself. Since the inner child visualisation on page 109, you have begun to visualise and explore the idea of the little you and gain more compassion for the actions that you took in order to try and protect them, and now you will explore what parts of yourself you have developed in order to carry out that self-protection. In the previous chapter, we also learned about the importance of self-compassion, and we will continue to develop that here.

> GROWING UP IN A DYSFUNCTIONAL ENVIRONMENT MEANT YOU HAD TO FIND WAYS TO SURVIVE. IT WASN'T SAFE TO BE THE REAL YOU.

There may not have been a physical threat that you needed protection from (though this may also have happened), but in order to be accepted within the family system you may have had to become a different version of yourself. Thinking back to the inner child visualisation from Chapter 5 and the dreams that little you had, we learned that you began to lose authentic you because you had to become different versions of yourself in order to survive within the family system. For example, if the true innate version of you was assertive and strong, the need for your toxic parent to stay at the centre of the universe will have meant that you had to be more of a shrinking version of you. Instead of feeling like you could assert your point of view into conversations, you learned to blend in at the expense of communicating authentically.

You will have begun to adapt almost from the moment you were born. Instead of being loved and nurtured into exploring and becoming who you are, you will have adapted in order to survive. At the heart of that will have been the need to protect the toxicity or dysfunction of one or both of your parents. In Chapter 1 we explored the traits of a toxic parent, how they make themself and their needs the centre of the household, and how everyone else must abandon themselves in order to protect this. It becomes the family's unwritten and unspoken rule, and it forces the children within the house to adjust accordingly.

If you have siblings, you may have different memories from your childhood and recall different perspectives from past experiences. It is not shameful to respond differently to those around you. There is a blind assumption that all children within a family setting are raised the same. In a dysfunctional family system this couldn't be further from the truth and, even in the most 'functional' of family settings, it is unlikely that children are raised the same. Even in a functional and healthy family, a second-born child's experience will never be the same as that of the firstborn. Their first steps are not 'the' first steps. Their first words are not 'the' first words. The firstborn had completely undivided attention in their initial years up until the second child was born – something the second child never experiences. I remember the midwife telling us we doted on our firstborn: 'Don't worry, the second one gets dragged up!'

She was joking, of course, but there was some truth in her jest. I hadn't fully understood what she had meant at the time, but having raised more than one child, I realise what the midwife was implying. With a firstborn your nerves mean that you pay attention to every single detail, fearing getting anything wrong. It just isn't the same with the secondborn; as much as you do try to treat them the same, it just doesn't happen.

These comments around siblings are common and accepted when talking about families. 'Middle child syndrome' or 'first-born syndrome' are common descriptors that separate siblings and highlight that there is a general awareness that children within the same family don't get the same treatment. I am a middle child and resonate with the traits of being highly competitive, a risk taker and a bit of a social chameleon, whereas a firstborn is more likely to be used to feeling the pressure of being the perfect role model.

I am not suggesting that any of this shapes who we are entirely, or that it is done deliberately, but simply that children are never raised the same, even when they grow up in the same household. If we add high levels of dysfunction and/or toxicity, siblings can have childhoods that are worlds apart. One sibling could reflect on a loving and nurturing childhood, while the other talks of toxicity and abuse. Both are telling the truth, and that's the important bit.

I have engaged with many services, from schools to charities and even children's services that work with young people, and sometimes there is no recognition of this whatsoever. Let me give you an entirely fictional scenario that is indicative of conversations I have had. A school asks me to engage with a young person, who is regularly acting up in lessons. Along with their one sibling, they come from a one-parent household, where the parent struggles with addiction. When I ask about why I am only working with the sibling who is acting out in school, the teachers will explain that the other sibling seems 'much less affected' and, in fact, has 'gone the other way'. This other sibling appears to be the 'perfect' child, well behaved and acing their exams.

Rather than evaluating both siblings' responses in the context of their home environment, there is a tendency to assume that one child is having a 'better' reaction, when in reality there could be a whole host of reasons why this could be happening. Think about some of the responses we explored in Chapter 4 where we looked at fixing, perfectionism and people-pleasing. In the scenario I just gave you, the child 'much less affected' is more likely abandoning themself in people-pleasing and perfectionism. Just because the response fits well with the schooling scenario, it doesn't mean that there will be no negative consequences in the long run. And let's be clear here, as we covered in Chapter 2, a toxic parent can and will actively treat their children differently, usually in an attempt to keep control. This will mean that, on the surface, one sibling could be growing up in an environment that offers no support whatsoever, while the other sibling seems to have the perfect environment. I must highlight here that both siblings are victims of the dysfunction in this type of scenario, and will both experience the negative impacts in the long run.

It is important that, having grown up in this, you are supported in seeing the full truth and context of your experience.

THE FAMILY SYSTEM

Before you explore some of the more unique versions of yourself that you will have become, there are some common roles within the family system itself that we need to understand. These are adaptive roles that children within a dysfunctional family system will take on in order to protect the main cause of the dysfunction – in your case, the toxic parent. Once in these roles, children within the family system keep them up in order to survive, and the parent's toxicity is protected. These are not consciously forced on the children by the toxic parent; they are adaptations by the children to the toxicity. However, the toxic parent benefits greatly as all their toxic behaviours are protected and even nurtured by the roles the children take on.

There are four main roles, and you may resonate strongly with one or find that you have moved through more than one of them or have held them all at the same time. In families where there are fewer than four children, some roles may not be filled, and children can play more than one role at the same time or move through them at different times. Even in families where there is only one child, they may take the weight of all the roles simultaneously or at different stages of their life.

The hero child

The hero child is the overachiever. As the hero child, you would have had glowing school reports every time, rarely got into trouble, and aced your exams.

You were the child that the toxic parent would always gloat about. You helped show the world that your toxic parent must be doing an amazing job. As a child, you lived with the pressure of making sure you matched up to this role. You would be very caring, looking after the other siblings of the house (if there were any). Your glowing school reports were full of stories of you being incredibly nice and likeable. Nothing will have ever felt quite good enough, though, and the perfectionism that we explored previously will have heaped pressure on your childhood.

As an adult, you may in some ways remain a high achiever. This might be in your career or perhaps in another way, like by living the 'perfect' family life as a doting parent or as a spouse in a marriage that has only ever been externally perceived as perfect. However, you are always left with feelings of guilt for never feeling fulfilled. Despite everyone loving you as a person and believing you have the perfect life, you are incapable of loving yourself or enjoying the life you have built. The core feeling that something is missing is one that is never too far away.

The mascot child

The mascot child is always the joker of the pack. Whether it was growing up at school or in your activities as an adult, making people laugh and turning even the most difficult of times into a joke are traits of the mascot child.

As the mascot child, you were the one that everyone in the family looked to when they need cheering up. You were forced to bring happiness to the household. It didn't matter if it was because of your toxic parent's mood swings and gaslighting (which we explored in Chapter 1), or simply the discomfort that was within the home, but the responsibility to make people feel better always landed on you. Emotional avoidance was one of the unwritten rules of the house, meaning any difficult feelings needed forcing under the carpet. It was your job to assist in this. You had to always be happy, funny and find ways to please other people.

As an adult, your personality is built around how happy you can make the people around you. As a result, when you are in the company of people who aren't happy, it feels like a complete character assassination. You can't shake feeling responsible for making sure everyone is having a nice time, and it means that you are almost incapable of communicating your needs through fear that they may upset others in some way. This is, of course, closely linked to the people-pleasing traits we explored in Chapter 5. The reason it leaves you unable to have your needs met is because your only goal is making everyone else happy. You will evaluate all the ways that you communicate and, if you fear that communicating your truth authentically will not improve the mood of those around you, then you won't communicate it, or you'll fabricate it to make it more fitting. You will have large social circles with lots of people who like you, and yet you'll still feel lonely most of time.

In your closer, more intimate relationships, you will work desperately hard to try and make sure the other person is feeling good all the time, despite this being an impossible task for anyone. Obsessively asking and checking that they are OK, being hyper tuned in to when they aren't and unable to remove the responsibility you feel to make it better. You may even find that when you cannot switch off from wanting to make them feel better, you cause arguments so that you can again work on making them feel better.

The scapegoat

As the scapegoat, you found yourself in trouble regularly, being almost drawn to chaos and feeling comfortable in it, while feeling like you always got the brunt of the blame for everything anyway. If there is a difficult family situation that happens in adulthood, you will notice that it is your name that is somehow shoehorned into taking most of the blame.

You always took the brunt of the family's difficult emotions. The toxic or dysfunctional parent cannot allow focus to fall on their toxicity, and their poor behaviour needs justification. Instead of looking at the true origin of everyone's distress, the family instead pointed to you, the scapegoat. The toxic parent will use the scapegoat time and time again to justify why they are the way they are. You will have been repeatedly told that the abuse and dysfunction only happened because of you. You will have subconsciously assumed this role, knowing that the way that you survive in that family system is to give reasons for people to use you as a scapegoat. As a result, you will often have been in trouble, perhaps even getting yourself into dangerous situations. The toxic parent then got to play the role of the victim and you were left with a feeling of 'what's the use anyway?'

As an adult, you may have struggled to shake that role and continued on a similar path of chaotic and self-destructive behaviour, but you are also a rebel in nature, willing to call out things that you believe need calling out. You don't want to follow the crowd and instead want to push against the common narrative. You find it easier than most to shoulder the blame in situations that aren't even your fault, because you have a sense of being used to it. You will find yourself being scapegoated in other scenarios outside of your family, whether that's at work, in your social circle or even in the wider community.

The lost child

As the lost child, you were quiet and unassuming, preferring to blend in and not be noticed. 'Shrinking', as we explored on page 103, is your most prominent trait, and you feel almost comfortable there.

Lost children are often the last born, and there is much less to say of this role as your duty was to simply blend in and not cause any problems. You were the expert at playing small and having very few needs. Your toxic parent will have often celebrated that you never brought any issues to the table, taking credit for this.

As a child, you lived a very withdrawn life, and likely still do as an adult, not wanting to burden anyone with any of your needs or wants. It may come across as a very relaxed and laid-back attitude when, in fact, it is much more about not taking up space. You try your best to blend in and not take up room in social situations. You're very agreeable and won't make any fuss unless pushed to. You may prefer being alone, or you may have built a social circle around yourself but are still hindered by fear of taking up too much space.

While we've learned how many of these roles manifest in more negative scenarios, not everything about these roles is bad and these behaviours are not necessarily something that you need to shake off. In fact, as with all versions of you (as you will discover within this chapter), there can be positives in them.

Personally, I identify with more than one of the family roles, but most stringently with the mascot child. Over time I have worked to integrate that role into who I am today. I enjoy the playfulness and humour that comes with it but remain acutely aware of the problems it can cause in my relationships when it does take over. This means that I can sometimes find it hard to communicate how I am truly feeling, opting to be sure the people around me feel comfortable. The paradox here is that, in most cases, this leads to my actions hurting everyone, including myself.

> YOU MAY FIND THAT YOU ARE STILL PLAYING THESE EXACT ROLES IN YOUR ADULT RELATIONSHIPS TODAY, OR YOU MAY HAVE MANAGED TO FIND SOME FREEDOM FROM THEM. IT IS ESPECIALLY COMMON TO FALL RIGHT BACK INTO THEM IF YOU ARE EVER AROUND YOUR FAMILY.

This will likely resonate with you. That part of you takes over and you adapt to surviving in the situation. 'Survival' is the key word here, a clue to what you are about to learn about all versions of you.

As well as the roles that you took on to survive within your family system, different versions of yourself will have become more prominent and have had a huge impact on how you experience the world. These versions present in different ways in your life. For example, they make you act in a different manner in different situations, almost like you have more than one version of yourself. Your personality can change, even your language and how you interact with others can shift as you become these different versions. In some cases, it is more like another part of you that lives in your mind, constantly talking to you internally and dictating how you should act.

THE INNER CRITIC

One of the most common and easily recognised versions of you is what most people call the 'inner critic'. You probably have one. I know I do, and it has been louder than usual writing this book. A dysfunctional childhood will often lead to a very loud inner critic. It may even have the voice of your toxic parent. The inner critic will play a huge part in all the traits you explored in Chapter 5. Whether it was the fixing, shrinking or people-pleasing, the inner critic's voice will have made you feel you needed to do those things. That voice in your head constantly tells you that you are not good enough, says that you shouldn't jump that next hurdle or that you are not making your friends happy enough. It never goes away and, at times, can become paralysing. You spend your life trying to shut it up, only for it to become stronger and more polarised. Most advice out there tells you to keep trying to silence it, but your inner critic never leaves.

JOURNAL PROMPTS

- Do you recognise your inner critic?
- What do you think of that part of yourself?
- How do you react to your inner critic when it comes up?
- Can you think of any positive reason why your inner critic might exist?

The final question might be the hardest for you to answer. How could a voice in your mind that is so critical of you have any kind of positive intent? I felt the same about my inner critic (and many other parts of me which we will go on to explore), but after finding the work of Richard Schwartz and the Internal Family Systems model, that began to change. His work showed me that if I looked hard enough, all these versions of myself had positive intent behind them, and that intent was to help me survive and try to protect myself. They were versions of me that loved me enough to try to protect me.

Looking back at how you answered the journal prompts just now, how difficult does it feel to start looking for that positive intent in respect to the inner critic? I ask that you trust the process here and, even if it feels a stretch to believe it, can you hypothesise? I realised with my own inner critic that it was so terrified of shame, it did everything it could to try to prevent me from getting into situations where I might be at risk of experiencing it. My critic's goal was to protect me, even if how it showed up actually caused me more pain. Recognition of this can help with the self-compassion that you have developed for some of the mistakes you have made. Your inner critic wants to protect you. If you can see it as another version of you, then it becomes easier to understand why it gets louder when you try to shut it up. It is a part of you whose only job in most cases is to avoid shame. If you try to silence it, of course it is going to get louder. This is the reason that having no compassion for and trying to rid yourself of your inner critic is the wrong tactic, and ultimately makes things worse.

Rather than fighting against your inner critic and wishing

it would shut up, can you become curious about why it is showing up and explore how you can make it feel safer and less scared of the shame? Can you remind it that you are not a defenceless child anymore, and that you now have lots of power at your disposal? You will find that the more that you do this, the softer the inner critic becomes. Not only will you then have compassion for it, but you can even become grateful for its existence. This softer version of the inner critic will help you to be the best version of yourself without paralysing you.

By now seeing your inner critic through a lens of curiosity, you will see it has helped you get to where you are. You will no longer hate it as a version of yourself, but know that it is a part of you that you need to work alongside so that it doesn't become too scared and start to run the show. When you live your life in harmony with it, it will help enhance your life, pushing you when needed without becoming completely overpowering.

The inner critic will be one of many different versions of yourself that exist. You will have many more to discover. Just like the inner critic, these versions of you are trying their best to protect you in some way, but often cause you more issues and pain. They may show up as different versions of you that you fall into, or as other, perhaps stronger, voices in your head guiding you. To get a clear understanding of these versions of you, it is worth visualising them almost as characters. This may initially feel a little 'out there', but doing so can really help your awareness of them and ultimately help you to reach the same place of connection and understanding of their existence. To highlight exactly what I mean, I want to show you some examples that are based on parts of myself that I have discovered. You don't have to identify entirely with any of them, but I want you to see how I articulate them, so that you can later reflect on some of the versions of yourself that you have.

VERSIONS OF YOURSELF

The tough one

The tough one might dress with attitude. Their resting face could be tense and angry. Their language may be spiteful and derogatory, and they always talk about how they have won fights or altercations. There say they are not scared of anyone. If you have a part of yourself that is similar to this, it will come out in times of fear. I have a version of myself like this that tends to come out when I am around men. My experience of my dad has shaped the way I view other men and, behind this, there is a slight fear of them. I have a core belief that they will eventually hurt me – or people I care about – and so my tough persona is an attempt to protect myself. If you have a part like this and it becomes too polarised or takes the reins too much, it will push people away and not allow for any type of intimacy. The positive intent here, though, is protection. It is a version that simply believes that offence is the best form of defence.

The intellect

The intellect might be smart in the way they dress and in their all-round presentation. They are always keen to talk about the books they have read and the wisdom that they possess to separate themself and behave slightly above everyone else. If you have a part of yourself like this, then it will take over when you have a sense that you are inferior in some way. I have a similar version of myself to this. I remember it being prominent when I first started working with corporate companies as a facilitator, helping their employees to develop resilience. What drives this is a belief that I am not good enough and so I must prove I am by showing my intellect as much as possible. I would find myself creating opportunities to quote books I'd read and would even notice myself trying to articulate words in a way I felt was more intellectual. When this version becomes too overpowering, you are much more likely to experience forms of burnout as you push and push yourself to prove your worth. The positive intent here is again linked to feelings of shame and believing that, if this part of you didn't exist, you wouldn't survive in situations where you feel inferior – much like my workplace example.

The loner

The loner is dull, bland and always looking to blend in. I picture them wearing drab colours and having no interest in leaving the house. They talk about how awful and dark the world is, and how it is not worth having friendships or being close to anyone. This is a version of you that is most likely to take over when life feels overwhelming. My version of the loner doesn't like me interacting socially, and will always give me reasons and create excuses not to call or text friends, or to resist working on my relationships – even with the people I care about. The loner believes they are not good enough, and that in the end people will only hurt you. 'What's the use anyway?' is a line I hear this version of myself saying on repeat. The positive intent is to try to protect you by preventing situations where you might get hurt.

The catastrophiser

The catastrophiser is a small, shaken and extremely nervous character. I imagine them with their arms folded, biting their nails, eyes darting from person to person and on high alert. This version of yourself is paralysed by 'what ifs', too scared to do anything, and is always looking for the worst outcome in every life scenario. This character will show up most prominently when there are big life decisions to make, or if you make any attempt to be spontaneous in some way. It will make you believe that everything is too risky and that you should stay in your lane and not take risks. My version of the catastrophiser is one that is often strongest on holidays and days out with my family. As a dad of six with my youngest being only six years old, even the smallest hiccup is a catastrophe. When I'm planning these days with my family, the catastrophiser in me will have me desperately believing I shouldn't organise them at all, feeding me all the reasons why they're a bad idea. The catastrophiser tells you everything comes with too much risk of pain and discomfort. The positive intent of the catastrophiser is in trying to avoid risk that will result in hurt. When it is acting too strongly, it can prevent you from doing anything or going anywhere in life, instead believing the next catastrophe is imminent.

The dark fire

This is a darker, more difficult version to comprehend – and this is by design. This is a more deviant version of yourself and even feels less human. I imagine this character as a dark, shadowy figure with fiery red eyes, but your version may be more like Wednesday from the *The Addams Family* or the Joker from

Batman. It may show up when things are going well or even perhaps in times of struggle. When this version of myself is present, I feel extremely anxious in my body and it forces me to seek escape in addictive behaviours, as we looked at on page 106. This character believes that life is only ever going to cause hurt and that happiness should be avoided as it will only, eventually, lead to more hurt. As such, its positive intent is to help escape the pain that comes with emotions. At its worst, it will have you engaging in behaviours that only ever exacerbate your struggles through its belief that life is too painful.

As I previously mentioned, you don't have to relate fully to these examples, and you may not relate to some of them at all, but hopefully they outline how you can have different versions of yourself that take over at different times. These versions of yourself are often trying to protect you, based on a belief that you are still the same age as when they were first needed. For example, when I was a highly sensitive young boy who wanted to cry a lot at school, the tough one would take over and prevent the shame I would feel from crying. My intellect version took the reins in my initial school years when I realised that intelligence could help me seem likeable in situations where I felt anxious. Finally, the dark fire makes perfect sense when placed in the context of my life. The unpredictability of my dad's alcoholism and his subsequent death when I was young will have created a deep-rooted fear of loss in me.

Becoming curious about the versions of yourself that exist and then exploring what their positive intent is can you help you to find and build more compassion for yourself in the moment. You will begin to realise that all these versions of you have helped you navigate your life up to this point. You can then begin to build a relationship with those versions of yourself to live a more integrated life.

You may sometimes feel like you are not being authentic when a different version of yourself takes over. Let's say that in your career, the tough one takes over and you speak to someone in a manner that you wish you hadn't. You may have even asked yourself in the moment, 'Who did I just become?' With this new way of viewing yourself in moments like that, you can start to see that version of yourself taking over and still remain in control. You can self-reflect and let that version of you know that you welcome some of its assertiveness, but that it doesn't need to take charge.

Another example might be in the way you interact with your catastrophiser, if you have one. Instead of letting it get completely out of hand and prevent you from doing anything, you could take a moment to make it feel safer. You could let it know that you are not a child anymore and that you have the tools to navigate the potential outcomes if things go wrong. Again, you are not creating more fear by trying to get rid of them, but rather helping them to feel safer so that they can relax and not take over.

If you can keep an open mind and explore the different versions of yourself, learn more about them and start to understand how they manifest in different situations, you will begin to gain a deeper, more empathetic understanding of yourself, and harness the ability to use these parts in unison. Together, they can become a powerful tool in all aspects of your life, from using your tough one character to assert yourself at work to using the catastrophiser for meticulous planning and accounting for every eventuality.

EXERCISE: VERSIONS OF YOURSELF

You are now going to start exploring parts of yourself. Reflect on the examples that I have given on the last few pages. You may have personas that are very similar to these, but you will also have other parts of yourself that are completely different. We are all unique people with different versions of ourselves.

As you reflect on the questions in this exercise, be creative and allow yourself to have some fun. The idea is that you can give each part you discover an identity so that it becomes easier to connect with.

Let's begin. Can you name and describe three versions of yourself?

Once you have identified the versions of yourself that you can picture most clearly, I want you to explore not only how they show up but also what they are scared of. Remember, the key here is to work towards developing compassion for them. I have listed some prompts below to help you with this, each with an example beneath to help guide you.

What is the name of this part?

The catastrophiser

What does it look like?

Biting nails, arms folded

When you think of this part, where does it activate most in your body and how?

I feel . . . My chest is . . . My tummy is . . .

What is this part trying to achieve?

It stops me from . . .

How does it protect you?

It helps me to . . .

What is its negative impact on you?

I cannot . . .

What does it say?

'You should . . .'

What is it scared of?

It's scared that . . .

What does it want?

It wants to . . .

What does it feel?

Worry, fear

What is its core belief?

It believes . . .

What does it believe would happen if it didn't exist?

It believes . . .

Once you've completed this reflection for one part, use the same prompts to explore the other two versions of yourself you identified earlier in this exercise.

You will now have explored three parts of yourself, but you will have more. Perhaps take the time now to explore every part of yourself before moving on. The more versions you find and the more you are able to connect with them, the more self-aware you are going to become. It is important to stress that you are trying to find out why they exist, and then how you can work with them by trying to run your life in a more self-connected way.

Some of the versions that you discover will likely be parts you have spent a lot of your life trying to bury or eradicate. Many self-help exercises encourage this, but this one is different. The more you learn about these other parts of yourself, the more you will be able to work towards a more free and empowered life. You can draw on the various parts that exist and work together in life. As crazy as it may sound, I often regularly hold an internal check-in with all the parts of myself that I have discovered. After a breathwork session, when I am internally reflecting, I will usually visualise each part of myself and see how they are showing up. Are they strong and overbearing? What are they scared of, and how do I remind them that I am no longer a defenceless child and that as an empowered adult I now have lots of things at my disposal? In doing this, I help to keep most of those parts of me feeling safe, as if we are integrated and working together.

In this chapter, you have further discovered that the ways in which you have shown up to life have been in order to survive the situations you faced. Although in many instances the versions of you that have taken over have ended up causing more harm than good, you can now see that they had positive intent and that with your new-found understanding you can make them feel safe enough to not go to the lengths that cause you harm. From here on, in time you will notice more parts of yourself showing up. Each time they do, you can get to know them deeper, find their positive intent, and learn to work with them. Take some time to now reflect on the work within this chapter and bring it all together using the journal prompts below.

JOURNAL PROMPTS

- Which version or versions of yourself have been showing up strongest in recent months?
- What can you learn about how you have seen the world as a result?
- What version of yourself do you become in relation to your toxic parent, both in their company and when you think of them?
- Has your view of yourself changed as a result of the work within this chapter and, if so, how?
- How and where can you create some more time to be more connected to the versions of yourself that you have discovered?

Breathwork

Now that you have become much more aware and connected to more of the versions of yourself, it is time to complete the conscious connected breathing routine and visualisation. Within this visualisation, you will meet with some parts of yourself that you have explored and it will help you become even more connected to them. Use the QR code below to complete this before moving on to the work in the next chapter.

8.
HEALING YOUR RELATIONSHIPS

Healing a relationship with a toxic parent is something that's too difficult for most people to comprehend. In most cases, when the parent is toxic, we are talking about healing a relationship that is not repairable. Your parents brought you into this world; they were meant to keep you safe, to love and nurture you into becoming the best version of yourself. When those very people create a lifetime of toxicity and abuse, the level of internal pain this creates is devastating and, in so many instances, that alone makes it completely irreparable. If you are still dealing with toxicity, healing can feel completely unreachable. It cannot be allowed to be that way for you.

YOUR HEALING CANNOT BE DEPENDENT ON THE ENGAGEMENT OF SOMEONE WHO SIMPLY WILL NEVER HAVE THE CAPACITY TO ENGAGE IN ANY TYPE OF HEALING. YOUR ONLY CHOICE IS TO FIND SPACE TO HEAL

WITHIN THE PARAMETERS OF WHAT YOU HAVE.

This might not mean repairing the relationship so that it becomes one that it is equal to the average parent–child relationship. It may even involve drawing a line under it. This might be the only way to heal from the relationship. The ideal scenario would be one where both you and your toxic parent come together and reflect on everything in full, with complete honesty, and work towards healing the pain they caused. Even if your toxic parent is still alive, with their traits that you have explored in depth now, they are almost certain to never even begin to engage in that way.

This is where so many people get stuck. They obsessively chase a relationship with their parent that their parent will never be able to show up to. Everyone, including people who haven't grown up with a toxic parent, romanticises what relationships should look like. We do it with all relationships. We read and watch fairy tales and dream of our love playing out in that way in films, where characters go through turmoil but run off into the sunset in happy endings. But this is idealistic, even in the most functional of family systems. Believing that real life can work this way is problematic, especially when you are dealing with a relationship with a toxic parent. By now, you have probably let go of your fairy-tale ending, but are you still clinging to the idea of a relationship that will likely never come? In this chapter we will dive deeper into self-love and its importance, before focusing on your relationship with your parent, looking at how you view them and where you can take your power back.

JOURNAL PROMPTS

Take some time now to get clear on where your relationship with your parent is today. Use the journal prompts below to do this.

- Describe what your current relationship with your toxic parent is like.
- If your parent were capable of changing entirely, describe how you dream of that relationship looking.
- Assuming that your parent will never change, and placing your needs first, describe what the best possible relationship you could have with your parent would look like.
- Think of the person that you love the most and describe what your advice to them would be if they had the same relationship with a toxic parent as you do.

Reflecting on these things is about giving yourself clarity. It is important to understand that you are not always trying to get somewhere. Healing isn't always about moving on to the next stage of being better. In fact, that's part of what you need to heal from. In any relationship with a toxic or abusive person, you are the victim. This is magnified even more when the toxic and abusive person is your parent. Yet, still, you have found the courage to focus up to this point almost entirely on the things that you can control. This is about getting clarity in your mind of your experiences and the impact they had on you, and being able to feel you have the power to navigate them in the best possible way for you. This is nothing short of what you deserve.

SELF-LOVE

Before you dive into healing the relationships with your toxic parent, let's explore self-love. When one truly loves and accepts themself, they possess a fearlessness in how they express themself. They have an underlying belief that they are worthy of the things that give them purpose in life. They recognise that they are enough exactly as they are, without the belief that they need to get to the next phase in order to be lovable. We discussed authenticity in Chapter 7 and, when someone loves themself, they are truly authentic as there is no fear of what others will see. Most importantly, it is innate. You are born with your value and so you are born with your love for yourself. Self-love isn't something you should be teaching yourself. It's not even something that you learn at school. Self-love is something that should have been installed in you from the day you were born by those whose job it was to make you feel safe and loved and able to become exactly who you are. Self-love should have been born out of the love in those relationships, but for you it wasn't. If it was, you would not have hidden from all these versions of yourself that you have discovered – and those versions wouldn't be working so hard from a place of fear in order to protect you.

The previous two chapters have been a deep dive into your relationship with yourself. As a result, you will have begun to develop some self-compassion and become more connected with yourself. If that hasn't happened yet, a regular practice using the visualisation from Chapter 7 will help you to develop some deeper love for yourself. In Chapter 3, we talked about how you built a fortress around yourself in an attempt to protect yourself. That fortress served its purpose, until you began to know you needed freedom. Until now, we've focused on dismantling that fortress and rebuilding it in a new way. Getting to this point is a good indicator that there are at least parts of you that love yourself enough to know you deserve more. Look at what you have done so far. You have reconnected with your body, begun to build a sense of community, looked at the patterns within your mistakes, developing your self-compassion in the process, and then gained a deeper understanding of the versions of you that exist. This is the kind of work someone would put in for someone they love, someone they want to build and nurture a relationship with. It's an incredible achievement for anyone, let alone someone who has grown up with a toxic parent. This isn't even your first attempt, either. Something you'll discover is that you have loved yourself all along. Growing up within the environment you did means that you simply didn't know what self-love looked and felt like.

Love is a by-product of the actions that you take. The mistake that people make is that they think simply bettering themselves will lead to self-love. The underlying belief is that if they can become good enough, they will be able to love themselves. If they just get to the next rung on the ladder in their career, earn enough money or meet the right person, then something will click and they will love themselves. Self-love doesn't work like that. Self-love is innate because your value in this world is innate. Your value exists because you exist. Self-love comes when you remove the things preventing you from seeing that value, not when you believe that your value is dependent upon the next step forward. Your love for yourself should be unconditional, as the love from a parent should be. It is no wonder that you became so detached from your value when your toxic parent's love was extremely conditional.

Of course, when you do love yourself, you will do loving things for yourself. When you do this, it will certainly help you on your journey to self-love, but if you don't go through the process of the work then it becomes more toxic positivity as we explored in Chapter 1.

JOURNAL PROMPTS

- Describe the way you feel about yourself right now.
- Look at all the work you have done up to this point both in life and within this book - what do you think that says about self-love?
- If you were to continue along this path, what would life look like in one year? And in five years' time? Ten years' time?
- Think back to that little you that you have discovered. How would they describe the person you have become throughout this work?

It's OK if you still feel some way away from loving yourself. It took years of survival to close yourself off from it; it will not necessarily come flooding back in a heartbeat. The important thing to understand is that it is about reconnecting internally with the little you and finding times and places in your life where they can feel safe and free. Healing your relationships in the way that you are about to is the final leg of this journey, before you go and get that little you once and for all so that you can become their champion.

Healing your relationships is the last big barrier. Until you can do this, they will loom over you and prevent you from truly developing a loving relationship with yourself. But before you panic, the work in this chapter is not focused on reconciliation with your toxic parent. As you explored in Chapter 2, whether you reconcile the relationship or not is entirely a personal decision. It is not one that anyone else gets to decide. It is a major flaw of society and Western ideals that, for some reason, children of toxic parents are always the ones pushed towards mending a relationship broken by the toxic person's behaviour. You are still expected to be the instigator of mending the relationship, irrespective of the level of toxicity or abuse. This is not OK and is not what we will do in this chapter – self-abandonment in order to mend someone else's toxicity will certainly not be forced on anyone. I will again stress that every situation is individual and constantly evolving, and so you have to do what is right for you. I will not be forcing you to instigate reconciliation of the relationship in that way.

That said, you need to find a way to heal that relationship. For some it will mean burying it once and for all, drawing a line in the sand and moving on. For others, there will still be the possibility of a relationship but with some adjusted expectations. Either way, we are not looking to place blame here; this is about understanding and getting freedom from the bonds of what is a very tangled relationship. Until those relationships and all the resulting emotions are untangled once and for all, freedom to develop a relationship with yourself is simply not possible.

I truly believe that your formative years, especially your relationships in those years, play a huge role in how and why you show up in the way that you do. The perfect childhood doesn't exist, and our experiences in our early years affect us all, but growing up with a toxic or dysfunctional parent means that these experiences have a far greater and more negative impact that extends into adulthood.

It seems to be an unwritten rule that exploring your parents' failings and their impact on you is the ultimate act of betrayal. In fact, even to think about the negative impacts of your parents' actions can leave one steeped in shame. Regardless of the level of dysfunction or toxicity, you are forced to frame your childhood experience in a way that dresses your parent in the best possible light. To do anything else would leave you open to others' negative judgement. This can be catastrophic for people like you who have been deeply impacted by a parent in so many ways, as it forces you into silence in an attempt to avoid that judgement.

PROTECTIVE FRAMING

I had always framed how I saw my dad in a way that was digestible for me and for anyone that I might have had to talk to about him. I can see now that I did this to people-please, in the same way you have already explored. I didn't want people to feel uncomfortable or be upset by my experience, so I would dumb it down for their benefit – and mine, too. This is common for those who have grown up with high levels of dysfunction. As you have explored across previous chapters, people look to avoid discomfort in a number of different ways.

One method I see all the time, particularly when it comes to family, is protective framing. It becomes apparent when people first start waking up to the realisation that their parent wasn't as perfect as they have let themself believe. For those who have had a toxic parent it is prevalent, and the framing they use can be split into three general groups. In many cases, people will move through these three, starting at the first and then slowly waking up to the reality.

The perfect childhood and the hero parent

This is when people frame their childhood only as 'perfect' and their parent is placed on a pedestal as a hero. From the moment you were born, your parent becomes a god-like figure to you. For those initial years every child is completely dependent on their caregiver. Your very existence is entirely dependent on what they do. This is why attachment to them is important for survival. In most cases, until you at least start school, you will not have had much else to compare your experiences to; your view of your parent was your view of the world. In order to attach to them, you had to adapt to what worked for them.

Every child needs support through every experience until they are old enough to support themself. With a toxic parent with the traits we listed in Chapter 1, we know you didn't receive this, but you likely still held your parent in high regard, at least for a period of time. It was in essence your only choice. As you began to develop the ability to rationalise your experience, you had to see your parent as a hero. To see the truth would have been too painful to bear. As a child, fully acknowledging the truths you have explored throughout this book would have been catastrophic for you. Looking at the emotional avoidance we've explored, the key defence in your childhood home was to pretend everything was OK no matter how bad it got. There was a complete avoidance of anything remotely uncomfortable – emotional avoidance at its finest.

The toxic parent will have painted themself as the hero throughout your childhood, too. There will have been lots of turmoil, perhaps your parent ended up parenting on their own or had been in very toxic relationships. They will have painted you or at least one of your siblings as being desperately difficult, thus helping to keep themself as the victim and at the centre of the universe.

The victim role they played and their constant recital of this will have made it extremely difficult for you to explore the reality of your experience. Not only that, but the common wider societal narrative is also that you should accept all your parent's flaws. The difficulty in this is that this might hold some truth if you weren't dealing with a toxic parent.

Combined, this can lead to the 'perfect childhood and hero parent' narrative being one that is desperately difficult to break, even well into your adulthood. Many adult children stick with this narrative right through into later life. In many cases people feel this is the only narrative they can keep publicly, even if they have moved beyond it, as they may be ostracised by people for speaking their truth.

Good enough childhood and good enough parent

This is where you have some awareness that your childhood was 'different', but no full admittance of the severity. This is often the second stage of awareness. You're normally made more aware of it as you share stories of your childhood and start to realise that things weren't quite right. If you have children of your own, you may realise that you wouldn't dream of allowing many of the things you experienced to happen to your children. Maybe you find yourself telling stories as funny anecdotes only to recognise other people's reaction is confusion rather than laughter. In this phase, you become more open to seeing things more truthfully, only to follow up with a strong defence – usually something like, 'But they had it really tough and were doing their best.' In this phase, you see closer to the truth of the situation but still need to be protective of the narrative of a 'good enough' parent and childhood.

Again, this is a very protective and, in most cases, needed phase: as you gently peel back the layers, you slowly open to the truth in a way that is manageable. The reasoning in this phase, that your parent did the best they could, is not always wholly untrue, but the way that belief is used is key.

Total acknowledgement of toxic childhood and parenting

Finally, you can recognise your childhood experience in its entirety and process the full level of toxicity. For many, this stage comes after healing work leads to discovery, or perhaps over time you have begun to piece together just how toxic an environment your childhood was. This phase is frowned upon by people in general. You will be scapegoated for speaking this truth. Even people in the 'healing' or 'self-development' space will suggest that you need to do more work to see things in a more 'loving way'. They are wrong. Depending on your experiences, you may reach a place that resembles that, but it is not an absolute – whereas recognition of your truth is. This phase is a difficult but very powerful stage to reach. There is no right or wrong to what you do with your relationship with your parent here, but, armed with the full truth, you are much more equipped to make the decision that is correct for you and where you are.

As is often the case, you may relate to all of these types of protective framing. You may have even gone through all three and found that you align most strongly with one of them. Everyone's situation is different, and so what is going to work for you is that which is right for you and no one else. I do want to encourage you within this chapter to really explore the third phase and seeing your truth in your experience. As we explored in the body first approach, you cannot be fully in your body and avoid your truth, however painful that it is. Discovering the full truth of that experience must happen if you are to break free from your toxic parent and reclaim your story. It is important to highlight that your truth is your truth, nobody else's. As you explore your experiences of life, your truth is also allowed to evolve, change and even return back to a previous truth. In fact, you should expect this to happen when on a discovery of yourself in the way that you are. You will have framed so much of what happened to you in a way that helped you survive. You recognised this in the previous two chapters when looking at what drove your actions in inventory and then when learning about all the versions of yourself. When it comes to your parent, in order to protect yourself from the painful truth of how they treated you, you will have created many different protective framings.

JOURNAL PROMPTS

- Being honest with yourself at this point, what protective framing stage do you think you are currently in?
- If you have been in more than one of these framings, what moments or experiences caused you to change?
- Are there any relationships now that you force into a certain protective framing today?

It is remarkable how many adult children of toxic parents find themselves stuck in the perfect childhood scenario. This is often a signal that they are not connected to their body and require a lot of spiritual and emotional bypassing. Again, this thinking isn't something to be scoffed at; it makes sense as a survival technique when there is often little other choice. When I think about my own perception of my relationship with my dad, I recognise how much it has evolved over time. I used to talk about the perfect childhood and wouldn't even mention my dad's drinking. Despite losing him to his own alcoholism, it felt too much of a betrayal.

The biggest problem with this is that it becomes impossible

to be in your body and be authentic. When you are framing your experience as perfect when it is was far from that, there are lots of feelings that stay trapped in your body and shape how you view the world without you even realising it. I used to 'passionately' discredit any talk that my addiction had anything to do with my childhood. I would shout people down, believing that it was coming from a place of self-knowledge. The opposite was true. It wasn't passion at all, it was defensiveness; I couldn't admit that childhood plays a role in addiction because it would mean looking properly at my own. I see this kind of scenario play out with many adult children of toxic parents. It can even seep into how they parent their own children. They can give them less love than they want to deep down, because if they were to do so, it would highlight the lack of love they received.

It is also common to move through the framings. I mentioned that people tend to move through the phases in the order shown, starting at the perfect childhood and landing at total acknowledgement, but flitting between them does happen. As you have just explored, being in that initial framing means a lot of bypassing, and that is not always easy to keep up. Life moments can pierce through it and the perfect childhood framing can crumble. However, it is often the case that when this happens, people work to quickly recreate that framing and get back into what feels like a place of safety.

Reaching total acknowledgement is not necessarily an easy place to stay either. It is a difficult truth, and the desire for even a good enough parent and childhood is something that never leaves people entirely. Rather than sitting with the uncomfortable truth, the mind will work hard to break that full acknowledgement. It will tell you that it wasn't *that* bad, that you're overreacting, and that there are people who had it way worse than you. Society will play a role here, too. Most people will tell you that 'life is too short' and that 'you'll miss them when they're gone'. Even people in the wellbeing space insist on framing your experience in a more digestible and less uncomfortable manner. This is why healing from toxic parenting is such a complex experience. There is always more than one truth. Total acknowledgement, coupled with further work, may bring you to a place of seeing what your parent did as good enough – but it also may lead to the realisation that it simply wasn't good enough and that the relationship is untenable.

Much of how you think and feel about your experiences probably remains in your mind and in your body. You have had little opportunity to explore it in its entirety. Even if you have talked about these experiences with someone who allowed you to, you will have likely still dressed up what you shared in certain ways to protect yourself from the feelings of betrayal that we have just explored.

YOU DESERVE THE OPPORTUNITY TO LET EVERYTHING OUT IN A COMPLETELY UNFILTERED WAY, AND THAT IS WHAT YOU ARE GOING TO DO.

EXERCISE: REFLECTING ON YOUR PARENTS

I want to encourage you now to get really clear on how you view your parents. It is important in this next phase to include all your primary caregivers who had an impact on your childhood, including any that you view as having a positive impact. This may include your mum and dad, stepparents, carers, grandparents and guardians. Start by making a note of who they are.

Next, you are going to use the four-second inhale, seven-second exhale breathing pattern that you are familiar with. I want you to sit or lie in a comfortable position and start the breathing pattern with your eyes closed. Then you are going to spend four minutes picturing each caregiver you have made note of. You can use a timer here so that you don't have to worry about when your four minutes are up, but it is important you do the exercise for at least that length of time for each caregiver. It may feel uncomfortable and difficult to keep your mind there for this long; whenever you notice it's getting difficult or your mind is wandering, simply bring your focus back to picturing that caregiver. Once the four minutes are up, answer the prompts below.

JOURNAL PROMPTS

- Where in your body was most activated during those four minutes?
- What words would you use to describe how you felt during that time?
- Can you summarise your view of the caregiver in two paragraphs or less?
- Do you feel like you are fighting against feeling any truths around this caregiver? If the answer is yes, what might they be?

EXERCISE: A LETTER TO AND FROM YOUR PARENT

I'd like to invite you to write a letter to your parents and caregivers from the previous exercise. Write a separate letter for each, putting down everything you would say to them if nothing else mattered. You are not going to send them this letter, so I want you to get everything out. This might include all the ways they have hurt you. You can talk about specific instances, and you can reflect on the impact they had on you.

Before you put pen to paper, there are some things to consider. I don't want you to overthink this too much. Get into the flow and let it out. Let go of the outcome or the idea that you have to reach a certain point - just get it out. If you feel like you have already said everything that needs to be said, this is different - I still want to encourage you to get this all out and complete this process. You may need to take some time with this exercise, though. It may bring up a lot for you, so be gentle with yourself along the way and take breaks when needed.

After completing your first letter, remember to consider who else you may need to write to. It's important to write a letter to every caregiver that you listed in the reflective exercise. Each person is just as important as any of the others, so you should still write letters for the parents or caregivers that you feel did an amazing job or who didn't cause you any harm. Contradicting emotions can and do coexist. You can feel desperately let down by someone you desperately love. You can hate something about someone without it taking away from how much you love them. I would take it as far as saying that if you have people in your life for whom you have no difficult feelings whatsoever, it is more likely that you don't want to see the emotions than it is that they don't exist.

This happens a lot with people and how they explore their difficult childhood experiences. They will take the more obvious reasons for their struggle and use those to shield them from some of the more complicated struggles. This is arguably never truer than for those with a toxic parent. You may be someone who has an incredibly toxic parent yourself and sees your other parent only in a positive light. I am not about to try and ruin that positive light, but it is worth exploring that relationship, too.

In my work, I often use the term 'phantom trauma'. It's a term born out of a medical phenomenon known as 'phantom pain'. Phantom pain is when an individual experiences pain that is physiologically not there. This imagined pain can be anywhere in your body and can especially occur after amputation. Similarly, phantom trauma describes people attributing their internal struggles to something that isn't the source of their pain and suffering. People take a single event and attribute all their struggles to that. They ignore some of the more nuanced emotional wounding that will have happened as a result. This can happen in obvious ways: perhaps someone grew up with a toxic and abusive parent but believes that their trauma stems from a single event at school when they were laughed at for an embarrassing moment. It is not that the experience at school wasn't traumatic and didn't have some impact, but in this case it is used in a way to protect that person from looking at the difficult truth. I have witnessed adult children of toxic parents do this.

A more subtle example of this same behaviour is when an

adult child of a toxic parent places every resulting feeling entirely on that toxic parent, only to go on to discover that some of their pain stems from feeling let down by the other parent, who witnessed the trauma happening but didn't do enough to try to prevent or stop it. Much like everything we have worked on throughout this book, phantom trauma can be a great survival technique, but only up to a point. Ultimately, it can also be a block to accessing the healing you need. If we look back at the previous example, it is not so much that you now need to bring all your focus to the other parent – the parent you feel let you down – and make them as culpable as your toxic parent, but it can be helpful to explore the roles of both parents, even if this is often much harder to do.

This was true in my own case. I began to attribute my pain to my dad's drinking. I would ignore the part of me that felt let down by my mum, too. It pains me to think this, let alone to write it down in this book. My mum is an incredible human, in spite of all the hardship she faced in life with my dad's drinking. Raising our family after his early death, she found a way. I have nothing but love for my mum and we remain close today. Having to explore the impact of her own mistakes was painful to do. But it was important. In doing so, it deepened my relationship with her. Rather than keeping these deep, difficult and resentful emotions buried in my body, they have been worked through and no longer have a hold on me. I am free to love my mum in the way I want to and in the way that she deserves as the incredible human that she is – mistakes and all.

So, writing letters to all your caregivers is important, and it really matters that you don't hold back. Until we find ways to complete the cycle of emotions and process them fully, your feelings remain trapped in your body and will come out in ways over which you have little control.

REMEMBER, KEEPING EMOTIONS IN DOESN'T MEAN WE ARE CONTROLLING THEM – IT MEANS THEY ARE CONTROLLING US.

Once you have completed your letters, I also invite you to write a letter back to you from them, saying everything you wished they would say to you. This is going to feel strange, but it is an important part of this process. Though I want to continue to let go of outcomes here, this will help relieve you of the responsibility you may feel for something that you should never have needed to. Write this letter as if your parent has broken free from their toxicity and is writing the letter that you deserve.

JOURNAL PROMPTS

- How did that feel for you?
- Were there any parts of you that you explored in Chapter 7 that were activated more?
- What did you feel in your body and where?
- Has your perception of your relationship with any of those you wrote letters for changed?

This exercise will have been a deep and emotive one. You may have been writing letters to and from just one parent, or you may have had three or four. Either way, it is likely the first time in a lifetime that you shared what has been trapped in your mind and body. The purpose of doing this is not for any fixed desired outcome. You will have found that it had an impact on how you frame your relationship with your parent. You can take strength from the fact that wherever it has taken you is much closer to the truth of where you should be. A reminder: this is about untangling so much of what is often left unsaid and unexplored in your mind. The healing of the relationship is about seeing it for what it is, recognising what is available from it, and adjusting your expectations accordingly.

It may be that writing the letters helped you to see some of the reasons why your parent is the way they are, and in turn this is softening how you see them. The following exercise may help you to further see them through a more human lens. If your parent is or was very clearly abusive, then this next exercise may not reap much reward. The reason I am stressing this is because I don't believe anyone who has been abused should be made to feel like they are failing, if they are unable to gain a better understanding of what led their abuser to abuse. The reason I still encourage you to go through with this exercise is simply to see what it brings up for you. Remember the analogy I introduced early on in this journey: how close can you sit to the fire without getting burned?

As I mentioned previously, we all see our parents in a godlike light in our early years. This can mean that you ignore who they are and spend your life expecting things from them that they simply will never have the capacity to give. This doesn't mean that you are not allowed to sometimes be upset or emotional about this, but until you find a way to adjust your expectations you are likely to grow resentful. This will then take up far too much of your head and heart space.

EXERCISE: ADJUSTING YOUR EXPECTATIONS

In the middle of a piece of paper, place a picture of your parent. If you don't have a picture, then just draw an outline of a person like the one opposite.

Write their full name at the top of the page. Down the left-hand side of the picture, write all the things they did or didn't do for you. Start every sentence with their name. On the right-hand side, opposite each point you have written, write the possible reasons why they did or didn't do the things you mention. You may not be sure in many cases, and if you're not then hypothesise.

You may write something along these lines:

Joe never cuddled me.	*Joe's dad never cuddled him and he didn't know how to express love.*
Joe always shouted at me more than my siblings.	*Joe was scapegoated as a child and has no idea how to process difficult emotions.*
Joe never told me he loved me.	*Joe doesn't know how to express love. His life has hardened him beyond this.*

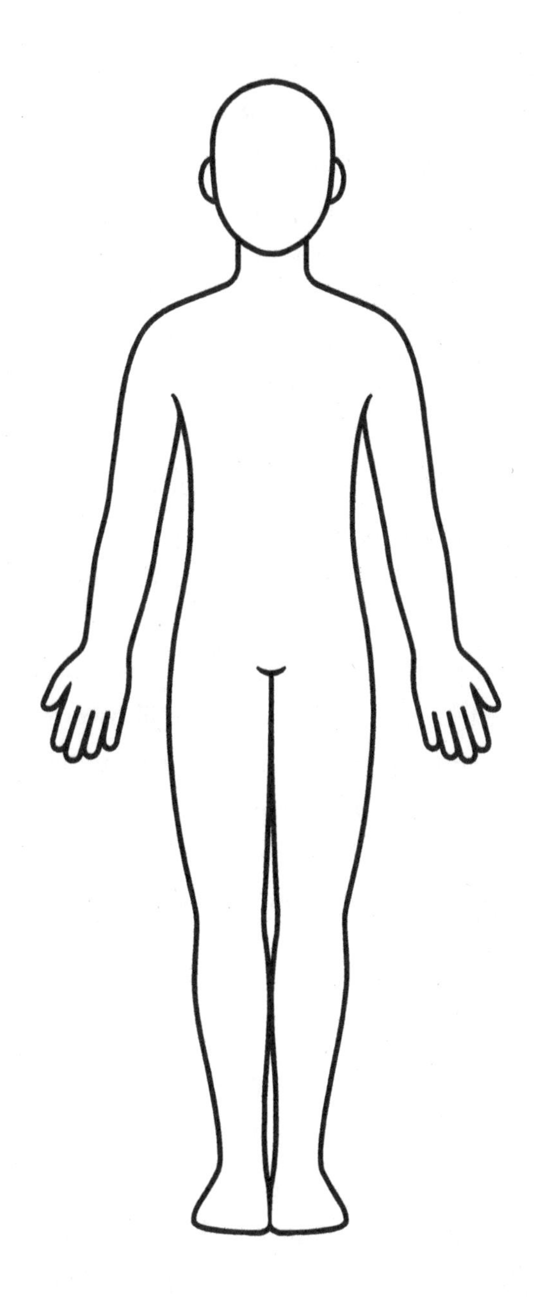

*

Completing the last two exercises will likely have brought up a lot for you. If so, this is positive. Remember what we explored with the body first approach in Chapter 4: this has been about completing emotional cycles, letting that emotion out rather than burying it down and appeasing everyone else. The breathwork will help to complete this cycle.

I want to stress once more that this chapter has been about taking responsibility for your life and the impact your relationships have had on it. This is not about taking responsibility for the abuse or toxicity that you faced, but rather no longer allowing them to imprison your power. Healing a relationship from one side is about making the best of an awful situation.

In this chapter you have explored how you have been on the journey of self-love, looked at how you will have framed your relationship with your toxic parent in a protective way, and allowed yourself to honestly express your true thoughts and feelings in regard to your relationship with your caregivers. Use the journal prompts below to bring this all together.

JOURNAL PROMPTS

- Thinking about all of the work that you have done up to this point, how much love can you sense towards yourself?
- Do you think work within this chapter has helped you reach total acknowledgement of your relationship with your toxic parent?

- Are there any changes you need to make to better adjust how your parent is in your life, regardless of whether you have cut ties or if they are no longer living?
- What would it take to finally draw a line and step away from the hold of their toxicity?
- Summarise how you now feel about your relationship with your toxic parent.
- Can you make a list of the special relationships in your life today, and why they are special?
- Imagine that little you: how do you think they would feel about you now?

You have done an incredible amount of work to reach this stage. Though the exercises may seem simple in nature, they often take you to profound discoveries. You will now have reached a much deeper and clearer understanding of how your parent's toxicity has shaped your relationship with them, and that is one of the key points here. You may have felt for a long time that so much of this was a 'you' issue. The realisation here should be that it isn't. If your toxic parent is still alive and you are still in contact, it will help to make some adjustments going forward. Recognise, also, that a toxic person of any kind will always try to have an impact, and so even though you are reclaiming power, you will need to be vigilant. You can use the letter-writing format again in the future if you feel you need to get things off your chest and know that saying them out loud will cause more friction and more reaction from your toxic parent.

This chapter may have changed the level of contact with your toxic parent that you now feel is acceptable. That is completely understandable based on the work. Hopefully you have developed some of the internal strength needed to be able to move forward with that when you feel ready. Think back to when you were setting the foundations for this journey and learned about the importance of community. You may need to draw on that more than ever in this instance because, as you adjust your expectations here, it may come with feelings of loneliness.

Breathwork

It is now time to complete the conscious connected breathing routine for this part of your journey. Once again, find some time to lie down and give your all to this breathwork. It will be followed as always by a powerful visualisation that will complete the cycle of the work that you have done within this chapter. Once you are ready, use the QR code below to complete the breathwork.

9.
BRINGING HOME YOUR INNER CHILD

When your inner child feels safe enough to connect with you fully, you clear the channel between your head and your heart, and the love you have always had for yourself can pour through.

Much like all the versions of yourself that you met in Chapter 7, your inner child has existed ever since childhood. It is the version of yourself that existed when you were authentically you, before life took hold and you began to adapt accordingly. Your inner child is innocent, free, curious and full of childlike wonder. The version of you that existed before you began abandoning yourself as you explored in Chapter 5, before the self-created emotionally avoidant narratives you learned of in Chapter 6, and before the roles you took on to survive within your family system as discovered in Chapter 7 still exists in you today.

You will have always had a sense it was there. You may have never recognised it as your inner child, but it is the part of you that you work so hard to protect. The part of you that has always felt alone and misunderstood. The part of you that you have almost never allowed anyone to be emotionally intimate with. There may have been occasions when you felt truly seen and safe with someone, when you felt like they could see all of you. Those moments happen when you are in the presence of someone that makes that little you feel safe.

YOUR INNER CHILD NEEDS REFLECTION

Before you began the work within this book, your life was still an attempt to protect the little you. At the hands of a toxic parent, you have been working as hard as you can to protect the little you, from the fortress you built around them to the versions of yourself that took the reins to steer you through. Somehow, some way, you've always found a means of protecting your inner child. But because you have been doing this unconsciously, eyes closed and with no awareness, it has left your inner child lost, lonely and disconnected from you. You may have caused harm to yourself and other people around you, you may have worked so hard chasing external solutions, or you may have simply withdrawn from society altogether, but the one thing all of this has done is almost completely sever that connection between you and your inner child. That is what this journey has been about. In order for your inner child to feel safe in your company, they need you to show up in your power. This doesn't mean you need to have everything figured out, or even be the best possible version of yourself. It just means that you can show up authentically and look them in the eye.

EXERCISE: VISUALISING THE LITTLE YOU

Let's take some time once again to visualise the little you. Sit or lie comfortably with a straight back. Close your eyes and take some slow breaths: inhaling through your nose for four seconds and exhaling through your mouth for seven. While repeating this pattern, gently picture that little you again. During the visualisation, I want you to get an understanding of what age that version of you is, and then what they truly needed from a parent. Once you've completed this exercise, move on to the journal prompts below.

JOURNAL PROMPTS

- What age is the little you?
- What did that version of yourself need from the perfect parent, if that were to exist?
- What does that version of you feel like now in your presence?
- When thinking about what they needed, feel free to also brainstorm some things they didn't need but which they still got. Some examples of needs might be things like connection and love, or more physical things like feeding and cuddles. Thinking about some of the things they didn't need, you could note things like being shouted at or made to feel like they were a burden, or being given too much responsibility.

With the work that you have now done on this journey, do you feel that you could give little you some of the things that they needed? In the previous chapters, you have set about working through everything that you have some power in. You have gained a clear understanding of the impact of a toxic parent and how to manage that. You have learned about the need to build a safe community around you and begun to lean in to that. You have embraced your body again and gained a better understanding of how you are truly feeling. You have taken responsibility for the person you are today and taken enough inventory to understand the things that drive the mistakes you have made. You have integrated more of the versions of yourself to reduce their fear and need to try. By this you have done as much healing around how you relate to your toxic parent as one can do without the support of the parent themself.

It is commendable that you have reached this point, and it means that now when you do connect properly with your inner child it will have much less fear and nervousness for you. You have done the work needed on yourself to be able to go and create a special relationship with that little you.

> YOU TRULY CAN BECOME THE PARENT THEY ALWAYS NEEDED AND DESERVED.

You will finally be able to look that inner child in the eye and fill them with a sense of safety. You know so much more about the parts of yourself and how you can call on them when needed in order to protect the little you. And you have the knowledge of your body to be able to start to trust your intuition again, so that you can trust what your body is telling you and do what is right for every part of yourself.

REACHING YOUR INNER CHILD

You have established that your inner child has been there all along, but simply trapped behind the walls of protection you have built up. You also have the recognition that they can now feel safe around the version of you that has done so much work on this journey. It is nearly time to reconnect with them fully, once and for all. As a result, you will re-establish that connection between your head and your heart, and allow true love to flow for every part of yourself – even during the most difficult of times. That little you deserves to have someone like you in their life to give them everything that they deserve, and you are now in a position to start to do that.

In this section, you are going to write two letters. The first one will be a letter from that little you to yourself. You will write this with your non-dominant hand – the hand you don't usually write with. This might be one of the tasks that feels strange at first – even silly – but the power that comes with writing with your non-dominant hand in this way is incredible. Some people believe that non-dominant-hand writing gives you greater access to feelings, gut instinct, inner wisdom and, in this case, your inner child. I remember doing this for the first time after watching some of the work of John Bradshaw, I didn't think it would have such an impact, but it was incredible.

EXERCISE: A LETTER FROM THE LITTLE YOU

In this first exercise, you're going to write a letter from the little you. Lean in to this and keep an open mind, being aware of what physical and mental sensations arise in your body and how they make you feel. The letter should outline a few of the wishes of your inner child. If your inner child got the chance to write a letter to you, this is what they would write. Your letter might look like this:

To older me,

I wish someone would cuddle me when I cry. I feel alone so much of the time. I wish someone could see how quickly I get overwhelmed, and help me. I just want to be loved exactly as I am.

From
Little me

With yours, you could use your name to replace 'older me' and 'little me'. So, as an example, mine would be 'To Josh' from 'Little Josh'. The above letter is just to help you get started. Be free flowing with it. You may write a much longer version as you lean in to this, or it may be similar in length to the example I have given. As always, there is no right or wrong here. You will write the letter you need to write.

Go ahead and write yours now.

JOURNAL PROMPTS

Having penned the letter, reflect on how it was for you using the prompts below.

- How did using your non-dominant hand impact writing the letter?
- What feelings arose as you wrote the letter?
- How do you now feel about going to save little you?

EXERCISE: A LETTER TO THE LITTLE YOU

Next, I want you to write a response to the letter. This time, you're writing with your dominant hand. I don't want you to get too hung up on the length, but ideally, this letter should be relatively short. It is more of a declaration to the little you of why you have been working so hard on yourself, and that you are now ready to come and get them to fully reconnect in a new and loving way. It should consist of a couple of examples of things you remember, and then some explanation of how you are going to come and get them and what this is going to look like. Here is an example of how this might look:

Dear little me,

I know better than anyone what you have been through. Like the times you used to sit at the top of the stairs worrying whether your mum was OK. Or the time you felt so much shame because of how drunk your dad was at the park.

I know you wished you could end it all, and I am so glad you didn't.

I want to come and get you. I want to bring you home with me and parent you in the way I know you have needed. I want to love you in all your emotions and cuddle you when you are sad and let you know that you are cared for.

I love you and I am going to care for you, and you will never need to try and fix me.

Love from
Me

As with the first letter, swap your name in to make sure it feels personal to you. If you begin to write and it does become much longer, that's OK too, but do make it clear in the letter and to yourself that there is a purpose to this letter – and that is to let them know that you are coming to get them.

Now, take some time to reflect on how that felt writing the second letter. What was it like to write to yourself with your dominant hand this time?

JOURNAL PROMPTS

- How does it feel to be the person you are now, making this declaration to your inner child?
- Describe how much love you feel towards the little you.
- List some of the emotions that came up when writing this letter.

So much of what you are told you need to do to find healing can become so extravagant and unreachable. You may even have your perfectionism convincing you that you need to do it better or work harder but, at its core, it can be so simple. You have likely felt guilt for how much you struggle or for reducing contact or cutting ties with your parent entirely, but meeting with your inner child in this way will show you that all you have ever craved is love. Love, and the presence of someone to witness you and hold you. The child that you were never had someone like you. They never had someone go to the incredible lengths that you have been willing to go to in order to finally make them feel loved. You have spent a lifetime of feeling lost and lacking in direction of how to truly meet the needs of who you are. You may have spent great amounts of money searching for something outside of yourself. You likely chased relationships and people in the hope that something out there would finally 'fix' you. Your inner child was locked so tightly behind the protective wall you built, never knowing if they would have a place to feel truly safe. Well, now they do have somewhere and someone to make them feel safe – and that is you. You are an adult now, you are no longer a defenceless child. Alongside the work that you have done, it is time to go and get that little you so that you can become their champion. The visualisation that will follow will be a huge moment on this journey.

Breathwork

There are purposely no journal prompts to close this chapter, breaking the mould of the journey so far. This is because the closing of this chapter is focused entirely on the reclaiming of your inner child in the visualisation.

The breathwork and visualisation that follow will be the biggest moments of this chapter and perhaps this book. Now is the time that you go and get that little you and bring them away with you. There is no need to reflect any further on the work that you have done. The visualisation will be a unique moment that many have said changed their life forever.

Use the QR code to take part in the biggest, most powerful breathwork and visualisation yet.

10. REPARENTING YOUR INNER CHILD

Everyone deserves a place they can call home. With the work that you have done on this journey, that little you finally has a place that they can call home and that's within you. You have discovered that your inner child has always been there and always been protected in some way by you. But now you have a relationship that you can now gently nurture.

The fundamental part of inner child work that is missing in most explanations is true connection with the little you. I am not talking about just visualising them in the way you have done on a number of occasions throughout this journey, but rather the clearance of the wreckage that was blocking the pathway from your head to your heart, as I explained in the previous chapter: the ability to be the safe, loving and nurturing adult that young version of yourself was always lacking. In becoming that, the connection is born. Now, as your inner child's true champion, you can become the loving parent they always deserved. This can be a lifetime's commitment.

THE FOUR PILLARS OF REPARENTING

You now have the connection needed to build and nurture a loving relationship with your inner child. Reparenting will mean building some daily practices with them. There are four key pillars to this: consistency, presence, freedom and emotional availability.

Consistency

Everyone, especially young children, needs and craves consistency. Consistency within a loving relationship helps evoke safety and build trust. Having gone from barely any connection whatsoever to having this new-found deep connection, it is common for most people that, at first, the consistency comes easily and naturally. Many people report being in almost constant contact and dialogue with their inner child after reaching this point in their journey. This is fantastic and, if you experience this yourself, I encourage you to run with it. However, be aware that over time, life can take over and what was once a natural and flowing dialogue becomes something that you need to attend to. You will need to actively create space in your life to ensure you keep this contact. I encourage you to create space for this now, rather than wait until it has dwindled too much. When this dwindling happens, you may find yourself needing to go back and redo previous parts of this journey. Think about what consistency will be right for you, and about creating an ideal consistency as well as a non-negotiable. For example, you may decide to have a brief check-in with your inner child every morning as well as having a non-negotiable ten-minute visualisation or internal reflection once or twice a week.

Presence

Presence is about the ability to truly be in the moment in any given situation. When explored fully, what any child really wants from those who should care about them most is presence. When someone is fully present with you, the sense of love and safety flows naturally. Being present with your inner child means actively giving time to witness them. Think about what you learned about the nervous system in Chapter 4. You will need to work to be in your relaxed state as much as possible. This is when you will feel calm and conscious, and when presence is more reachable. You are going to need to draw on your self-compassion here, too. For most people who grow up in dysfunction, and particularly those with a toxic parent, being in the relaxed state and cultivating presence is not always easy. You are going to need to explore what activities help to bring about that presence in you. It could be getting out in nature, engaging in creativity, or playing some kind of sport. Whatever it is for you needs to become more than just a pastime; it needs to become part of how you live.

Freedom

Freedom in this instance is about the freedom for your inner child to be exactly as they were born to be. You have gained so much knowledge around emotional avoidance, protective traits and the different versions of you, and it is unrealistic to believe that just being armed with all this knowledge will mean that the people-pleasing stops or your inner critic remains forever softened. The walls of your fortress will again begin to rise, and so moving forward you will need to make sure that your inner child and your relationship with them still has regular moments of freedom. True freedom in this regard will come when you feel you can be completely authentic, when the roles you play in life don't have much hold over you and the versions of yourself feel safe. You will need to think about how you can make this happen and about who in your life makes you feel like you can be this free. This is where the community aspect you began working on way back in Chapter 3 will become important. If you still don't have anyone in your life who makes you feel like your inner child has the freedom to be witnessed, this is something you should make a priority to explore. You will know when you have these people, as when you are around them with your new inner child connection, none of the versions of yourself will be overly activated or feeling like they need to protect you. You will simply feel free.

Emotional availability

Emotional availability is arguably the most important of all. It was the distinct lack of emotional availability from your toxic parent that ultimately severed the connection between your head and your heart and meant that you began to bury the connection to the little you. Now that you have this connection back, it is absolutely vital that you create emotional availability. Again, the body first approach becomes a vital practice. In order to be emotionally available for all parts of yourself, your body needs to feel like a safe place to be. This means creating regular time to complete emotional cycles, to listen to your body and know when it needs some release. As the adult child of a toxic parent, the fact is that your initial reaction in most moments of high emotion is to disconnect and push them down into your body. If you continue to let this happen without regular moments to allow some release, your body will quickly become a scary place to be, and you will once again break that connection between your head and heart. Your job here is going to be to think about what rituals are going to aid in this. The relationship that you have built with the breathwork could become very important here.

LITTLE YOU'S NEEDS

The four pillars will help you to bring focus to how you need to act within your new role reparenting little you. As well as that, you are going to need to make sure you are aware of their needs. Reflecting again on their age, it is helpful to think about what brought them joy at that time of their life. What personality traits did they have and – the deeper question – who were they before the life they were dealt began to change them?

EXERCISE: GETTING TO KNOW THE LITTLE YOU

Take some time to again visualise little you. Use the four-second inhale, seven-second exhale with your eyes closed and set a timer for six minutes. Spend this time picturing the little you in your mind again. Allow some space at the beginning, around five cycles through the inhale/exhale pattern, and then ask the following three questions on a loop, either out loud if that feels comfortable or asking them over and over in your mind:

What brings you joy?

How can we have fun?

Who do you want to be?

As you do this, be aware of what comes from the little you. Don't judge anything, just notice.

JOURNAL PROMPTS

Having completed the exercise, use the journal prompts below to capture what you learned.

- List everything that you know can bring your inner child joy.
- List everything that your inner child can do to have fun.
- List everything your inner child wants to be.

Most people, including those who grow up in what could be regarded as more functional environments, become disconnected from the essence of who they were. Having grown up with a toxic parent, this was magnified for you. Managing to reconnect with your inner child and realising the things they needed and wanted can have different impacts on different people. You may still find it difficult to access some of what your inner child wants or, if you can, you may still feel a sense of embarrassment at what comes up. This makes sense; you will have a had a lifetime of believing that survival was dependent upon hiding your needs, as well as having your needs devalued and even mocked by your toxic parent. You may have reached the stage where this all feels like a complete revelation too, and what your inner child needs pours out of you and you cannot wait to get to the regular practice of reparenting. It is really important for me to again highlight here that, wherever you are with this, it is not a reflection of how 'well' you have done the work. There are so many variables that can impact the experience you have, from distance from the toxicity in terms of time, to how easily a visualisation comes to you. What matters is that you are showing up and trying.

LITTLE YOU REPARENTING PLAN

'Be the parent you needed when you were young!'

I really do love this quote. If you have your own children, it's important you are the parent they need, not the one you needed, but I do think this quote sums up what reparenting is. You can now be everything you needed in a parent when you were young. You cannot go back and rewrite the past, but you can change what happens today and, with the work that you have put into this journey, you are more than equipped to give your inner child exactly what they need. Creating a plan is a great way of holding yourself accountable to showing up.

Here are some points to help get you started on your reparenting plan.

Daily acknowledgement

This is fundamental. As I mentioned when talking about consistency on page 197, for large periods moving forward you may feel that connection to your little you is constant. If so, that is fantastic, but don't rest here. Think about creating a daily acknowledgement. You could make this a two-minute stand-alone dedication with the sole focus being on your inner child, or you could weave it into something else. For example, when you are brushing your teeth, you could acknowledge your inner child, the benefit being that you will brush your teeth every morning and evening and so it can help set this practice in stone and mean missing the acknowledgement becomes much less likely. Another acknowledgement idea that I have witnessed lots of people do is to have a picture of their childhood self as their wallpaper on their phone, on their key ring, or stuck on the refrigerator as a regular reminder to acknowledge their inner child.

Inner child journalling

Journalling of all kinds is something that I would encourage everyone to do, but this is a slight variation. If you found the non-dominant-hand writing in the previous chapter powerful, then this could be a real game-changer for you. Journalling with your non-dominant hand as your inner child can bring about deep insight. It can help to invite you into the world viewed through their eyes and to get clear on their needs, and to what extent those needs are or aren't being met. This can be a highly emotive exercise, so it will be important to think about what consistency would be suitable for you if you choose this as one of your practices.

Letter-writing

Letter-writing is some of the most powerful reflective work that you can do. You have written a number of letters within this process and each one of them has played a huge role in untangling the emotions that lay trapped inside of you. Letters from the adult you to your inner child and then the writing from the little you to yourself in the non-dominant-hand format can be insightful. It doesn't have to stop there. You and your inner child can write letters that you don't send to anyone. An example would be one from your inner child to your parent. This could bring about some huge insight and potentially release more trapped emotions. You may want to make this one of your regular practices, or you may have it in reserve as something you use when you have a sense that the connection between your head and your heart is waning. It's important to remember here that you are not necessarily trying to land somewhere as a result, but rather are processing your internal struggles.

Identify fears

Identifying what scares your inner child can play a huge role in maintaining self-compassion. Remember, the different versions of you will become more activated and, as a result, harder to control when fear is higher. Spending time simply noticing will become one of your most insightful practices. Just noticing who you become in each moment and then being curious about what that is telling you. Maybe you notice your inner citric is loudest when you have to present at work and this tells you that, in that setting, you're still fearful that you are not good enough. Perhaps you people-please more around people that you care about the most. This shows that you still have a sense you must work hard to be lovable. Try not to judge yourself too harshly in these moments and see it as meaning that your fear is not irrational when viewed in the full context of your inner child and all the versions of yourself. Discovering your fears and keeping track of them can help you when interacting and reflecting with yourself. Instead of shaming yourself and beating yourself up for how you've reacted in certain moments, you can reassure yourself that you did your best with what you had, while also reminding yourself of the person you know that you can be.

Mirror work

As part of this journey, we looked at mirror work on page 117. Mirror work is a powerful way of piercing through any defences that you have built up. It is almost impossible to remain fixed on your own gaze if you are lying to yourself about anything. It can also be a gateway to your inner child and the connection you have with them. Regular mirror work is incredible for self-accountability, particularly if you use reflective questions alongside it. For example, you could introduce mirror work every evening before bed and ask yourself: 'Did I do right by me and all my parts today?' or 'Am I happy with the person I was today?' It is amazing what wisdom can come from this. However, be warned, it is often prone to unearthing uncomfortable truths! This is a practice that can be introduced with consistency. Personally, I find this to be a great daily morning practice.

Inner child visualisations

This is another practice that you have used on more than one occasion during this process. It is the perfect way to encourage yourself to be present with your inner child – removing all distractions and just reflecting is a simple but effective practice. The way you have done that within this journey has been to set a timer, focus on your breathing with your eyes closed, and picture your inner child in your mind, sometimes introducing questions to take it even deeper. The timer is important because it removes the concern of how long is long enough. You commit to a time and stick with it and see what comes up for you. There are other ways of doing this, too. Online you will find lots of different guided visualisations and meditations. These are particularly good for those of you who struggle with the silent reflections. As a practice, this is another that is best approached with some consistency. With visualisations and meditations, it is a bit like developing a muscle in that the more that you do with it, the more comfortable you will become with it and, as a result, the more powerful the potential experience will be. A key point to note here is that you won't have a huge experience every time. Annoyingly, it is one of those things that you may only realise the benefits of when you let the practice drop.

Inner child connection

This is a practice that may be a little harder to fulfil, but if you can find a way, it is powerful. Finding other people who have a safe and connected relationship with themselves will benefit you and your inner child immensely. You don't have to meet with people with your main intention being to let your inner child play with theirs – it is a little more subtle than that. When you are around the type of person who has that comfortable connection, you will find yourself feeling a much deeper sense of ease and comfort around them. Rather than working hard self-organising or keeping all the versions of yourself at ease, you will be free to be yourself. It will be as if the little you gets to wander freely. Be gentle with yourself during this practice, though, and know that it will come when it comes and that you don't have to force it. Doing so with the wrong people could result in creating more fear.

Continued inventory

In Chapter 6, you learned about inventory writing and the profound impact it can have on self-understanding and self-compassion. I cannot encourage you enough to make this a continued and consistent practice. This is the regular practice of checking in with yourself and the mistakes that you have made, looking at what drove them and what you could have done better. Like all the practices, it is important to not do this one from a place of shame. The purpose is not to highlight how flawed you are so that you can try and metaphorically beat it out of yourself, but rather to be aware of who you are and how you can keep your side of the street clean. Inventory can often produce some much-needed actions, too. For example: it may help you to see where you need to make amends to someone. It is also great for helping you spot when a version of yourself has taken over and needs some interaction to reduce their fear and soften. As mentioned, this should be a consistent practice. I would suggest making it a daily practice, with a minimum of three times a week being non-negotiable.

Joy

I have purposely titled this practice as one simple word: joy. It's fascinating to recognise that this is almost the forgotten practice in many healing and wellbeing spaces. Creating and finding moments of joy is the single most important practice you can develop. It is not as simple as it may sound, though. As the child of a toxic parent, you will almost certainly have forgotten how to allow yourself to have joy. You will feel uncomfortable in it, or not allow yourself to be in it at all. You may even discover a version of yourself that could aptly be named 'the killjoy' that you may need to visit and redo some of the work from Chapter 7 with. But with your now-clear pathway between head and heart, can you start to lean in to joy? Using the reflection you previously did in this chapter, where you explored what brought your inner child joy, can you find some experiences that allow you some freedom in your joy? Once you have found them, make them consistent. Find small spontaneous moments of joy as much as you can, too, but make a consistent practice with the sole focus being joy. Even a healing journey can become the very thing that stands in the way of your joy. It is common to get so locked in to the belief that you need more healing that you miss so many natural moments of joy, as well as prevent yourself from actively creating them. It is time to make joy a priority.

As well as the practices that I have listed above, you may discover more that work for you. Nothing should be off the table here, and you should go out and explore every possibility with an open mind. When stripped back, reparenting your inner child is about being totally there for yourself. It is about understanding your innate value and recognising that you deserve to be loved in your entirety. In having the focus of nurturing and reparenting your little you, you are, in turn, loving yourself.

You are now going to bring this all together and create a reparenting plan. For this, you will create and implement a daily practice as well as some regular non-negotiables. Your daily practice will ideally be a morning and an evening routine. It needs to be achievable, so don't make it too outlandish or it will fall away quickly. Your non-negotiables will be your practices that you never miss. They are as important as the air you breathe and the water you drink.

First, look at the lists you created at the beginning of this chapter for your inner child's joy and what they would like to be. Create at least three new practices from these. For each one, decide on regularity. Will they become a daily routine, or will they be a regular non-negotiable? Here are some examples:

- *Creating art. At least once a week I will dedicate one hour of time to getting lost in creating art.*
- *Walking in nature. I will take a one-hour mindful walk once a week in nature with no device.*
- *Words of loving affirmation. Every morning I will use words of loving affirmation to my inner child for two minutes.*

Once you have this list, take into account all of the work that you have done throughout this journey, the four pillars introduced in this chapter and the examples of reparenting techniques to create your own reparenting plan. This should consist of clear daily practices and a group of non-negotiables. Here is an example of how it might look:

Daily Routine

Morning (before any other daily activity):
Acknowledge my inner child through three-minute breathing, eyes closed and visualising all parts of myself including the little me.

Evening (before going to bed):
Do mirror work for two minutes, including inner child affirmations, followed by reflective inventory without pen or paper.

Non-Negotiables

- *Thorough inventory with pen and paper every Sunday evening.*
- *Playing guitar once a week for a minimum of thirty minutes to bring my inner child joy.*
- *Full conscious connected breathwork session twice a week to complete emotional cycles and ensure I can remain 'body first'.*
- *Check in once a week with someone I trust to hold me accountable.*

You now not only have a connected and meaningful relationship with the little you, but you have begun to equip yourself with the knowledge and plan needed to continue to nurture that relationship by reparenting. This reparenting can become your life's work and will always be something that you know you can reconnect with when things feel like they are slipping. Your reparenting plan can and should evolve over time and is something that you should be evaluating regularly to ensure you don't fall into the trap of going through the motions too much. Be aware that this will inevitably happen. The trick is to notice the warning signs, and revisit this work to reinstate what you know is effective. Your little you is very lucky to have someone like you who is willing to put in the work needed.

JOURNAL PROMPTS

- Looking at your reparenting plan, is there anything missing?
- Does it feel manageable?
- Write a statement of commitment to yourself and all the versions of yourself, committing to your reparenting journey, and sign it.

Breathwork

Once you have completed these journal prompts to close this chapter, it is time to complete the final breathwork of this journey. This one will be a celebration of the journey you have been on and a recognition of your new-found powerful relationship with every single part of yourself - but most importantly with your little you. When you feel ready, follow the QR code and lie down once more for this breathwork session.

CONCLUSION

You came here with at least an inkling that your toxic parent was preventing you from living the life that you deserved. You were lost, confused and unsure that you even possessed the power that you needed. Now, not only have you found the power to reclaim your story, but you also have a place you can finally call home – and that place lies within you. You get to be the one that sits that little you on your knee and tells them you are proud of them. You hold the self-awareness needed to make every single part of yourself feel safe enough to allow you to be the architect of your own life. And, most importantly, you have cleared the pathway between your head and your heart so that self-love can flow freely. As a result, when you look in the mirror, the person staring back at you is one that you can feel proud of.

YOU ARE YOUR INNER CHILD'S CHAMPION.

You get to show the little you that they are worthy of love, connection and support, and as a result you are loving yourself. Self-love is the by-product of the actions you take, and you have taken those actions in abundance.

This journey began by confirming what deep down you already knew: that your parent wasn't like the fairy-tale version you see in the movies, and for reasons that remain irrelevant, they couldn't be what you deserved. When you can, revisit Chapter 2 and reflect on how you will manage the situation in the moment moving forward. No longer will you approach situations that involve your toxic parent as if you are still a defenceless child: you now know that you have much more at your disposal. Boundaries will become easier to set and a sense of self-worth will mean they become easier to stick to as you celebrate the person you become.

Looking back at Chapters 3 and 4, community will be something that you can continue to develop in a way that feels right and manageable to you. You can trust yourself more now, you are more in touch with your needs, and so you can grow your community in a way that suits you. What is common to recognise for those who have truly found themselves is that a smaller, tighter, more trusting circle is what works best. That includes people who truly allow your inner child to feel free in their presence. When you find connections like this, nurture them into bonds because they will become so important. Your body first approach will mean that you can now trust your body in what it tells you. Your intuition becomes your greatest asset. If your body doesn't feel right in the company of someone else, no longer will you automatically fall into people-pleasing or shrinking, but rather you will listen to your body and take the action that is needed in the moment. Knowing how to listen to your body in this way will be key to knowing yourself.

You learned the importance of starting in the now. Though a struggle in the moment nearly always has its origins in something in the past, you now recognise that the work needed must start with how you are showing up today, and then work backwards. Your new relationship with all of yourself will help in this, and will also support you in maintaining your self-compassion. The recognition that self-compassion comes naturally when you are able to see your experience in its entirety is what will stand you in good stead here. Yes, you will strive to learn from your mistakes and try to do better in future as a result, but you will also hand yourself the recognition of understanding what drove you in the moment, and that it doesn't automatically mean you are a bad person. Committing to a regular inventory of some kind is going to be a game-changer in your life moving forward.

Understanding all parts of yourself is something that most people mention as being the work that really changed how they see themselves. It helps to create a revolutionary way of self-reflecting, one that can empower you to remain in the driver's seat in moments that would have previously overwhelmed you. As time goes on you will discover more versions of yourself that aren't yet clear, and this will only serve to deepen your understanding of yourself. Meet with all versions of yourself as much as you can from this point on, and always remember that your aim is to help them all feel safe in being a backseat passenger in your life. The moment any of them begins to take the wheel, remember not to fight them but to come back to compassion and curiosity as fast as you can. This is when you will create safety and help the versions of you soften, bringing you back in control.

Healing your relationships was no easy task. As I mentioned in Chapter 8, in an ideal world you would work towards resolution of some kind, looking for common ground. When dealing with toxic people, this simply isn't possible. Thankfully, your healing from the impact of those relationships does not have to be dependent upon engagement from the other person. Once again, you found the courage, and you found a way. There is often no fairy-tale ending when it comes to relationships with toxic people. At least, no fairy-tale ending in the way you might think. The most important relationship in your life today is the one you have with yourself, and that is one that you have now created beyond what many people believe is possible.

> YOUR RELATIONSHIP WITH THE LITTLE YOU WILL BECOME THE MOST IMPORTANT RELATIONSHIP IN YOUR LIFE.

By keeping the pathway between your head and your heart clear, you will always be in touch with your inner child. As result, you will always have access to your innate value and power. Work as much as you can on your reparenting plan, ensuring that you are working on yourself as the parent in that bond as well as giving your inner child the things they need to feel safe. This will be a daily practice. I wish I could tell you that you will now run off into the sunset and never struggle again, but that would be a lie. In fact, without being too clichéd, this is the beginning of a new journey – and one that most definitely won't be linear. All the exercises that you have completed within this journey are ones that you can revisit regularly, and I would encourage you to do so. You will now also have a relationship with the breathwork that means you can tap in to it whenever needed. I would encourage you to actively create regular space to do breathwork sessions as this can help to clear out your emotions.

We never reach the destination of being fully healed but, with the right amount of self-awareness, we can spend our lives moving towards healing. My experience has been that the moment that I think I have finally figured it all out, I'm back at the beginning of another cycle and I have to take myself back through all of the work. If nothing else, remember the struggles you've had were never yours to carry. You didn't ask for this, you didn't do anything to deserve it, but you and only you have the strength and courage to face yourself, and to face the toxicity of the very person who was supposed to make you feel loved in order for you to find freedom in your life. Many people who complete the process outlined in this book return to go through the work in its entirety on a regular basis. Once a year is common, but I would suggest that whenever you feel like life is once again getting away from you, you can once again revisit it.

JOURNAL PROMPTS

Before my final reflection I will leave you with some evocative questions to answer on paper. Explore these in as much depth as you can.

- What has been the biggest learning for you?
- What do you want to leave behind for good?
- What are you most grateful for from this journey?
- How can you ensure your reparenting plan stays in place?
- Write down all of the reasons you love yourself.

My hope is that with this book you have rediscovered your innate power and feel that you can now navigate life in a way that suits you and helps to make sure that your needs are still met. My wish is that you now see clearly that you were never broken. You will never be somebody who needs fixing; what you really needed was to reconnect with your inner child and every single part of yourself. Go forward in life now with the knowledge that you can look yourself and everyone else in the eye, knowing that you cared enough about yourself to work through the discomfort that most people can't even bear to glance at. When things go awry, remember that you have a plan. You know the path, and your inner child is always there waiting for you to be their champion.

MOST OF ALL, BE PROUD.

Be proud that you cared enough about yourself and your future to stand up and break a cycle that has likely existed for generations. Pain travels down through generations until someone is willing to do the work. Despite the fact that it was never your burden to carry, the person willing to do the work was you! Your story is now your story, and the toxicity no longer imprisons you. It was always them, not you!

FURTHER RESOURCES

Books

Adult Children of Emotionally Immature Parents by Lindsay C. Gibson
The Body Keeps the Score by Bessel van der Kolk
Chasing the Scream by Johann Hari
Healing the Shame That Binds You by John Bradshaw
Hold On to Your Kids by Gordon Neufeld and Gabor Maté
Home Coming by John Bradshaw
In the Realm of Hungry Ghosts by Gabor Maté
Lost Connections by Johann Hari
No Bad Parts by Richard C. Schwartz
Self-Therapy by Jay Earley
When the Body Says No by Gabor Maté

Speeches

'Healing the Shame That Binds You' by John Bradshaw
https://www.youtube.com/watch?v=UBAAgdRHW1M&ab

'This could be why you're depressed or anxious' by Johann Hari
https://youtu.be/MB5IX-np5fE?si=ShKz0hq0FwpFihKF

Charities and organisations

Anxiety UK
https://www.anxietyuk.org.uk/

CALM (Campaign Against Living Miserably)
https://www.thecalmzone.net/

Mind
https://www.mind.org.uk/

Nacoa
https://nacoa.org.uk/

Samaritans
https://www.samaritans.org/

Young Minds
https://www.youngminds.org.uk/

INDEX

abandonment of self 34, 61–2, 99–108, 138–9
  see also people-pleasing
acceptance, need for 113
acknowledgement by adult child
  of inner child 203, 210
  of toxic parenting 171–2, 174–5
addiction 78, 106–7
  alcoholism 57, 107, 123, 174
adolescents *see* teenage experience of abuse
adult relationships
  'fixing' mentality 82–3, 101–2
  with inner child *see* connection, with inner child; reparenting (inner child)
  kindness from others 21
  people-pleasing 2, 87–8, 99–100, 168–9
  shrinking into background 103–4, 146
  effect of suppressed emotions 84
  with toxic parent 26, 39–45, 50–1, 214
  in trusted community 64–8, 214
  usefulness to others 15, 94
  see also relationship healing
adulthood (of child)
  boundaries 45, 46–53
  decision-making 17
  dreams not realised 95–9
  effect of child roles 143–4, 145
  parental abuse 39–45
  personality 147–54
  protective traits 168–74
  recognising and expressing abuse 34–6
  rights and core values 47–9, 50
  see also adult relationships
'after everything I did for you'(guilt-tripping) 40–1
aging parent, reactions to 45
alcoholism 57, 107, 123, 174
ambitions not realised 95–9
anger
  not permitted in child 14
  precipitation in child 25–6
apologetic behaviour 104
attainment of child
  celebrated only in public 19–20
  impossible standards 18–19
attitudes to toxic parenting 11, 31–2, 168, 170

authenticity 111–14, 164
see also abandonment of self; versions of self
avoidance of emotions 72, 73, 88–9, 124–8, 170

betrayal, sense of 16, 30, 168, 175
birthdays, manipulation through 27
'black sheep' position 27, 34, 66
blame
'scapegoat' child role 144–5
and self-compassion 132–3
body connection
body sensations 70, 71–2
breathing exercises 86–7, 89–92
lost in childhood 80
and mirror-reflection 118
and protective framing 173, 174
body first approach 71–3, 214
body sensations 70, 71–2
boundary setting
for grandparents 45
guidance 49–53
rights and core values 47–9, 50
bravery, encouragement to 'be brave' 72–3
breathing techniques 7–8, 81, 86–7, 133, 176, 210, 216
conscious connected breathing 7–8, 90–2
guidance (link) 37

caregivers 175–6, 177–8
'catastrophiser' version of self 152, 153, 155, 156–7
'centre of the universe' view *see* narcissistic behaviour (self-centredness)
character assassination *see* personal attacks; smear campaigns
childcare, from toxic grandparent 41, 44–5
childhood memories, recalling and hypothesising 112–13
closing statements 51–2
coercion *see* controlling behaviour
comedian role in family 143–4
community of trusted individuals
creating 64
expanding in healing process 65–8, 214
connection
with body and emotions *see* body connection
with inner child 167, 191–5, 206–7
with versions of self 150, 158
conscious connected breathing 7–8, 90–2
consistency, in reparenting 197–8
controlling behaviour
emotion control 12, 13–15, 72
gaslighting 17–18, 72, 84
grandparents 41, 44–5
guilt-tripping 21, 40–1, 50
invisibility to outsiders 11, 12, 13, 19, 25, 32, 39
oversharing with child 15–17
personal attacks 21–2
reactive abuse 25–6
reconciliation pretence 42–3
through siblings 42, 43–4
the 'silent' treatment 41–2

smear campaigns 26–7, 44–5
spiritual bypassing 23–5
threats 22–3
through written communication 16, 27, 40, 42–3
coping mechanisms
addictive behaviour 106–7
'fixing' mentality 82–3, 101–2
fortress mentality 56, 56–65, 68, 165
helping others 107–8
hiding emotions 14, 108–9
hypervigilance 23, 76–7
people-pleasing 2, 87–8, 99–100, 168–9
perfectionism 102–3
shrinking into background 103–4, 146
see also versions of self
core values, in setting boundaries 48–9
co-regulation 77–8
creative activities 209, 210

daily routine (reparenting) 210
damage to self *see* abandonment of self; controlling behaviour; invalidation of experiences; self-hatred; self-sabotage
'dark fire' version of self 153–4
decision-making, impact of toxic parenting 17
defamation of child's character *see* smear campaigns
denial of toxicity
in gaslighting 18
by others 11–12, 19, 25, 32, 39
by siblings 43–4
digital communications from parent 16, 40, 42–3
disconnection 72, 73, 77
see also avoidance of emotions; connection, with inner child
dreams of another life 95–9

emotion of child, control by parent 13–15
emotional availability, in reparenting 199–200
emotional avoidance 72, 73, 88–9, 124–8, 170
emotional engagement
and authenticity 111
avoiding with parent 50–1
through body connection 86–7, 89–92
see also connection, with inner child; reparenting (inner child)
emotional expression
avoidance 72, 73, 88–9, 124–8, 170
denied to child 14, 72, 77
high arousal under stress 76–7
in later relationships 88
in reactive abuse 25–6
suppression 72, 84
emotional instability (mood swings) 22–3
empathy for self 117–18
escapism 107–8
exercises
body first three states 85–6
on caregivers and parents 175–6, 182

exercises – *cont.*
conscious connected breathing 91
inner child 109–10, 125–7, 189, 191–4, 200–1
mirror-reflection 117–18, 133, 134, 205
personal inventory 130–1
versions of self 156–7
expectation adjustment exercise 182

families
'black sheep' position 27, 34, 66
extended family 27
position of child in family 140, 146
relationship with other parent 16, 178, 179
roles in dysfunctional families 141–6
sibling perspectives and treatment 42, 43–4, 139–41
fears
of inner child 204–5
of parental reactions 20, 76
feelings
hiding 14
in nervous system states 85–6
see also avoidance of emotions; emotional engagement; emotional expression
first-born children 140
'fixing' mentality 82–3, 101–2
forgiveness
of parent 120–2
self-forgiveness 122–3, 124–5, 134, 135
fortress mentality 55–6, 165
learning to share 60–4
urge to rebuild 68
framing of experiences 168–74
freedom, in reparenting 198–9
friendships
and 'fixing' mentality 82–3
effect of people-pleasing 100
reviewing and developing 65
effect of smear campaigns 27
see also community of trusted individuals

gaslighting 17–18, 72, 84
generosity, as a parental weapon 20–1
good enough childhood/parenting 171
grandparents, toxic parents as 41, 44–5
guilt-tripping 21, 40–1, 50

healing process 2
dismantling the fortress 56–65
expanding community 65–8, 214
letters to/from parents 177–81
recognition of abuse 34–6
see also relationship healing
'hero child' role 142–3
'hero parent' framing 169–71
hiding
of feelings 14
of inner child 108–9
of self (shrinking) 103–4, 146
hypervigilance 23, 76–7

ingratitude, used as weapon 21, 40–1

inner child ('little you')
acknowledgement of 203, 210
fears 204–5
hidden away 108–9
importance of relationship 216
journalling 203
joy for 208, 209
letters to/from 125–7, 191–4, 204
loss of connection 188
mirror-reflection 205, 210
presence 187–8
reconnection 167, 191–5, 206–7
reparenting *see* reparenting *main entry*
visualisations 109–10, 125–6, 189, 206
inner critic 148–51
'intellect' version of self 151–2, 154
Internal Family Systems model 149
intimidation (threats) 22–3
invalidation of experiences
by others 11–12, 19, 25, 32, 39
by parental gaslighting 18
by siblings 43–4
inventory writing 130–1, 207, 210

jealousy, parental 18–20
'joker' role in family 143–4
journal prompts
abandonment and authenticity 114
adult management of parent 53
dreams of another life 96
empathy and acceptance 118–19
healing process 184–5
identifying mistakes and actions 132
inner child 110, 128, 189, 192, 194, 201, 211
inner critic 148
journey experience 217
letter 'from' parent 180
loneliness and connection 67
monitoring nervous states 75, 92–3
protective framing 173
recurrent scenarios 46
self-forgiveness and self compassion 134, 135
self-love 166
starting recovery 36
toxic traits 29
versions of self 148, 159
view of caregivers 163, 176
journalling, non-dominant hand 203
joy
for inner child 208, 209
not permitted in child 14, 208

kindness from others, lack of trust in 21

last-born children 146
'leaving the door open' ploy 42
letter writing
to/from inner child 125–7, 191–4, 204
to/from parents 177–81
life potential (dreams) 95–9

loneliness
  building trusted community 64–8, 214
  dismantling fortress mentality 55–6, 60–4
  from secrecy 55–6
'loner' version of self 152
'lost child' role 146

manipulation *see* controlling behaviour
'mascot child' role 143–4
meditation 90
middle children 140
mirror-reflection exercises
  to connect with inner child 205, 210
  for self-compassion 117–18, 133, 135
mistakes
  letter to inner child 125–7
  personal inventory of 129–33
mood swings 22–3

narcissistic behaviour (self-centredness)
  child's experience 13–14, 19–20, 99, 138–9
  towards adult child 40, 43, 52
nervous system, energy states 74–86, 92–3
non-dominant hand journalling 191, 203
non-negotiables (reparenting) 210
online sharing 66

other parent, relationship with 16, 178, 179
overachievers 142–3
oversharing with child 15–17

paired work in communities 65–6
parental failings
  in normal parenting 12, 29, 31
  recognition by adult child 30
  toxic parenting *see* controlling behaviour; personality of parent; toxic parenting; toxic traits
parental figures, in wider community 67
'peer' relationship (parent with child) 16
peer relationships (teenagers) 113
people-pleasing
  in family 143
  protective framing 168–9
  effect on self 2, 99–100
  in therapy 87–8
'perfect childhood' framing 169–71, 173–4
perfectionism 102–3
personal attacks 21–2
  see also smear campaigns
personal experience of author 3–6
  alcoholism 4, 57, 107, 123, 174
  childhood environment 112–13
  escapism 107–8
  as fixer of problems 83
  healing work 4–6
  life ambitions abandoned 98–9
  loneliness and sharing 57–60
  loss of father 72–3
  parenthood 58–9, 122–3
  protective framing 168–9, 173–4
  response in therapy 87–8

self-sabotage 106
versions of self 151, 152, 153, 154
personal information, right to privacy 50
personal inventory 129–33
personality of child/adult child
abandonment of self 2, 34, 61–2, 99–108, 138–9
in adulthood 147–54
child roles in family 141–6
protective framing 168–74
protective traits 99–108
personality of parent
jealousy and resentment 18–20
lack of self-reflection 24, 28–9, 40
mood swings 22–3
narcissism 13–14, 19–20, 40, 43, 52, 99, 138–9
victim mentality 28
'phantom trauma' 178–9
positivity without validation 23–4, 83
presence, in reparenting 198
projection by parent 22, 28
protective framing 168–74
public facade of parent 24–5, 42

random contact by parent 39–40
reactive abuse 25–6
reasoning with parent as an adult 51–2
reconciliation
with aging parent 167
pretence of by parent 42
recovery from abuse *see* healing process; relationship healing
reflection
for creating boundaries 48
reflecting on parents (exercise) 175–6
rejection
of child's success 18–20
personal attacks 21–2
through the 'silent' treatment 41–2
see also weaponisation by parent
relationship healing 161–87
problems of toxic parent 161–2
protective framing 168–74
reflection on caregivers 175–82
self-love 164–7
relaxed state (nervous system) 74, 75–6
returning to after abuse 82
religion 32
reparenting (inner child) 196–211
needs of 'little you' 200–2
pillars of process 197–200
plan 202–11
reporting of parental abuse 34
see also denial of toxicity; invalidation of experiences
resentment by parent 18–20
responding to abuse
avoiding emotional engagement 50–1
putting yourself first 52–3
recognising fixed nature of parent 49–50
response to 'silent' treatment 42
response to written messages 43
setting boundaries 46–9
sharing personal information 50
rights as an adult 47–8, 49, 50

'scapegoat child' role 144–5
secrecy
  and loneliness 55–6
  and shame 119, 126–7
self *see* abandonment of self; sense of self; versions of self
self-centred parental behaviour *see* narcissistic behaviour
self-compassion 116–35, 215
  identifying emotional avoidance 124–8
  inventory of mistakes 129–33
  self-forgiveness 122–3, 124–5, 134, 135
self-forgiveness 122–3, 124–5, 134, 135
self-hatred 122–3
self-love 164–7
self-reflection, absent in parent 24, 28–9, 40
self-regulation, lack of due to parenting 78
self-sabotage 105–6
sense of self
  and authenticity 111–14, 138–9, 164
  loss of 99–108
  in toxic environment 94
  see also abandonment of self; versions of self
sensitivity to mood 23
  see also hypervigilance
shame
  and denial of toxic parenting 33
  and exploration parent's failings 168
  felt by child/adult 14–15, 18, 34, 119–20
  and inner critic 149–50
  and secrecy 119, 126–7
  and self-talk 116
sharing with others 60–1, 65–6
shrinking into background 103–4, 146
siblings
  differing perspectives 139–41
  manipulation by parent 42, 43–4
'silent' treatment, effect of 41–2
smear campaigns 26–7, 44–5
  see also personal attacks
social media posts from parent 42–3
somatic practice 89–92
  see also body connection
speaking out
  effect of 28
  see also attitudes to toxic parenting
spiritual bypassing 23–5
stressed state (nervous system) 76–8, 84
survival state (nervous system) 78–9, 80

teenage experience of abuse
  parental jealousy 19–20
  reactive abuse 26
  smear campaigns 26–7
text messages from parent 16, 40
threats 22–3
'tough' version of self 151, 154, 155, 156
toxic parenting
  adult child acknowledgement of 171–2, 174–5

behaviours *see* controlling behaviour
and boundaries 45, 46–53
distinction from inadequate parenting 29
effect on nervous system states 74, 75–6
effect on relationship with other parent 16
experienced as an adult 38–46, 51
impact of term on adult children 35
public attitude 11, 31–2, 168, 170
scale of dysfunction 31
traits *see* toxic traits
toxic positivity 23–4, 82–3, 166
toxic traits
awareness of shared traits 30
emotion control 12, 13–15, 72
gaslighting 17–18
ingratitude accusations 21, 40–1
jealousy and resentment by parent 18–20
lack of self-reflection 24, 28–9, 40
mood swings 22–3
oversharing with child 15–17
personal attacks 21–2
reactive abuse 25–6
smear campaigns against child 26–7
spiritual bypassing 23–5
ulterior motives 20–1, 40–1
victim mentality 28
see also coping mechanisms
traits of toxic parents *see* toxic traits
trust in self and others
destruction 18, 27, 74
lack of 21

ulterior motivation of parent 20–1, 40–1
unpredictability (mood swings) 22–3
usefulness to others, in adult relationships 15, 94

validation of feelings 30–1
see also denial of toxicity; invalidation of experiences; positivity without validation
versions of self
as child within family 141–6
discovering as adult 147–59, 215
exercise 156–7
using visualisation 150
victim mentality 28, 170
visualisations
inner child 109–10, 125–6, 189, 206
versions of self 150
young child in distress 81–2

'walking on eggshells' 22–3, 76
weaponisation by parent 21, 26, 40–1

young adults *see* teenage experience of abuse

ABOUT THE AUTHOR

Josh Connolly is a resilience and wellbeing coach, leading conversations around addiction recovery and dysfunctional family environments. As a certified breathwork practitioner, co-host of the podcast *115 Miles* and founder of the Inner You self-healing programme, Josh's work resonates with people struggling to reconcile the past with the present.

Josh is also an ambassador for Nacoa – a national charity supporting people affected by a parent's drinking – and is an influential mental health advocate. He has appeared on the BBC, ITV and *Channel 5 News*, and on programmes such as *Victoria Derbyshire*, *Good Morning Britain* and *BBC Breakfast*.

ABOUT THE AUTHOR